Nurturing Your Baby's Soul

A Spiritual Guide
for Expectant Parents

Nurturing Your Baby's Soul

A Spiritual Guide for Expectant Parents

ELIZABETH CLARE PROPHET

COMPILED AND EDITED BY
Nancy Hearn and Dr. Joye Bennett

SUMMIT UNIVERSITY ◡ PRESS®

NURTURING YOUR BABY'S SOUL:
A Spiritual Guide for Expectant Parents
by Elizabeth Clare Prophet.
Compiled and edited by Nancy Hearn and Dr. Joye Bennett.
Copyright © 1998 by Summit University Press. All rights reserved.

Library of Congress Catalog Card Number: 98-60410
ISBN 0-922729-39-5

SUMMIT UNIVERSITY 🌙 PRESS®
Summit University Press and 🌙 are registered trademarks.

Printed in the United States of America
First Printing 1998

Parts of the present work appeared in a different version in *The Science
of Motherhood for the New Age*. Copyright © 1986 by Montessori
International.

Dedicated to all souls

waiting to be born,

to love and be loved,

and to fulfill their mission in life

Contents

ILLUSTRATIONS AND CHARTS

Editors' Preface

Have you wondered if there is anything you can do to increase your child's potential before he* is born?

Is it possible to commune with the soul of your child during pregnancy, or even before conception?

Do you have any influence over which child is born into your family?

Can you spiritually prepare to receive a soul with spiritual graces? or leadership abilities? or a scientific mind? or musical or artistic genius?

The purpose of this book is to answer these and related questions to help expectant parents understand the meaning of spiritual parenting before birth. This compilation interweaves two points of view on this subject.

The first is from Elizabeth Clare Prophet, who for many years has taught on spiritual issues related to conception, pregnancy and childbirth. The main text of the

---

*Throughout this book we have used the pronouns *he* and *him* in most cases to refer to the child in general. These terms are used for readability and are not intended to exclude females. We use the pronouns *she* and *her* to refer to the soul because each soul, whether clothed in a male or female body, is the feminine aspect of the masculine Spirit, or Higher Self.

chapters is composed of these teachings. They represent the core of her wisdom on parenting before birth, drawn from her unique perspective as a pioneer of practical spirituality and from her experience as the mother of five children. Many of these teachings were published previously in draft form or were available on audiotape; some are from unpublished sources.

The second point of view comes from a diverse group of parents who were familiar with Mrs. Prophet's teachings on pregnancy. We inquired about their pregnancy-related experiences and communications with their unborn children. We also wanted to know if and how they applied Mrs. Prophet's teachings to their preparation for parenting and whether they experienced benefits from spiritual practices before or during pregnancy.

Many of the parents we interviewed told us about special experiences they had had with the souls of their unborn children. And some related accounts of healing from their use of the spiritual practices recommended by Mrs. Prophet. With the consent of these parents, we have included some of their stories in this book. These stories are set in italic type. (Some names and details have been changed at the parents' request.)

Of course, not all expectant parents have such explicit spiritual experiences. The deep soul connection between the parent and unborn child is in many ways a mystery and often difficult to articulate. Some parents we interviewed could not initially think of a particular spiritual experience they had before or during pregnancy. Others were hesitant to share their experiences since they questioned whether their contribution would be helpful. But in reminiscing they often came to the realization that a seemingly mundane experience actually represented a profound connection with their child's soul.

As you read these stories and spiritually prepare for parenting, you may find yourself remembering or becoming more aware of your own special experiences with your child's soul before birth. We have included a number of blank pages at the end of this book so you can write down your reflections, thoughts, feelings, dreams, intuitions or spiritual experiences.

Even though we interviewed both mothers and fathers, most of the stories included in this book are from mothers. We simply did not find as many fathers who had stories to tell. However, those fathers who did communicate with us confirmed that the father's spiritual preparation for parenting and his involvement during pregnancy are as important as the mother's. Both mother *and* father can begin the bonding process with their child long before birth if they understand how to nurture, teach and communicate with the child's soul.

We would like to thank all the parents who contributed their comments and personal experiences. We regret that we were unable to include every account. From the shortest and simplest to the longest and most heart-rending, all were precious reminders of the blessings of childbearing. We would also like to thank the research assistants and editorial consultants who contributed to the creation of this book.

Nancy Hearn

Joye Bennett

Prologue: A Soul's Journey

Imagine this . . .

A soul in heaven is waiting to be born. She has already had her life preview with wise and loving spiritual guides. Together they worked out a specific life plan for her based on her greatest needs.

She has mixed feelings about her plan. She is excited about the mission of love and healing for which she has been studying and preparing. She can hardly wait to apply what she has been taught since her previous life on earth. She knows her parents and teachers will help her fulfill her mission. And most of all, she sees the effects of her mission touching hundreds, then possibly thousands of souls across the world.

Yet she has some apprehension and concern about her life plan. Her challenges in life will be difficult. But she knows that most of these challenges are simply the return of her own past mistakes coming full circle. Her compassionate guides have given her wise counsel to help her overcome these challenges.

She also knows that after she is born, her mission will become only a faint memory. She is keenly aware that she may be distracted from her mission, especially during her teenage years. She can't afford to lose any precious time and wonders if she will make the right choices along the way. But she knows that her friends in heaven will not desert her. And her guardian angel will always be there to guide and protect her.

As she looks around her at the wondrous beauties of her heavenly home, she tries to remember what it feels like to be in a physical body—especially as a helpless baby. She vaguely remembers how slow and heavy the earthly body feels compared to her light body.

And she thinks about her parents. Her spiritual guides have shown her specific experiences she had with the souls of these parents in previous lives. Her past experience with the soul of her father has been, for the most part, positive and harmonious. She takes comfort in knowing that.

Her mother for this next life was her daughter in a past life. Some painful scenes from that life still play before her mind. She was harsh with her daughter and often belittled her. Thus her remorse is deep, and she has agreed to be the daughter this time around. She will have to endure by her heart's love whatever hardship must come between them—and forgive.

In recent years, she has watched from heaven these two who are to be her parents. She watched as their paths brought them together in this life, as they courted, as they fell in love, as they shared their thoughts, married, established a home and hoped for children. She watched as they rejoiced when her mother's pregnancy was confirmed and then as they prepared a room for her, exulted in her growth in the womb, bought the sheets and blankets, the tiny clothes now folded, lying in neat rows.

Even now as she listens to their conversation about her birth, she feels their joy and expectancy. Her heart wells up with eagerness to live on earth again. To be with the souls of her parents again, her sister a long-lost friend, a brother to join them. And then much later, a family of her own!

Just now, everything is possible. She knows who she is, where she has been and what she needs to do. She knows her strengths and weaknesses and what she must overcome in this life. She knows she needs to repay old debts to some she has known before and will meet again.

She reflects on how long she has been waiting for the opportunity to be born again. And she thanks God for another chance to make things right.

Soon she will enter the birth canal. It will be scary, but she's done it before. It won't last forever. And then she'll take that first breath and be held close to her mother's breast.

She draws closer to her parents. She can't wait to smile at them and to give them all the love of her heart. How much she needs them!

It's almost time . . .

CHAPTER ONE

Your Child
Has a Mission

Our birth is but a sleep and a forgetting;
The Soul that rises with us, our life's Star,
Hath had elsewhere its setting,
And cometh from afar:
Not in entire forgetfulness,
And not in utter nakedness,
But trailing clouds of glory do we come
From God, who is our home.

—WILLIAM WORDSWORTH

Every soul enters life as a tiny babe in the womb. Before birth, the soul has full conscious awareness of who she is and what she has accomplished in past lives. Most important, she knows what she needs to accomplish in her next life to make the greatest possible spiritual progress. Thus, the soul's sense of identity is well defined and can sometimes be felt or experienced by the parents long before conception.

⤻

Before I conceived my first child, my husband and I were living in Italy. I had a dream that I was on a canal in Venice. But the water in the canal was solid ice and we were riding in a sleigh. All of a sudden, there was a little boy sitting next to us.

I suddenly woke up and said to my husband, "We're going to have a boy!" He asked if I was pregnant, and I said, "No, but we're going to have a boy." About eighteen months later I conceived, and a beautiful baby boy was born to us.

⤻

This experience occurred more than a year before my daughter was conceived. My future husband and

I were not engaged at the time and, as a matter of fact, our relationship was not going anywhere because we were working in different areas of the country. So, marriage was not something about to happen in my life.

On this particular night, I was sitting in my bed reading and do not recall what I was thinking about. All of a sudden, I heard the most beautiful light, angelic, joyous voice say with a flair, "Sarah!"

I repeated her name out loud. Then the voice said, "Sarah Marie!" And I repeated this to her. There was pure joy in her voice. It seemed presumptuous that this was a soul announcing herself to me since I wasn't married—but it felt like she was. I kept this in my heart for many months.

By and by, my future husband and I got engaged. I told him the story about Sarah and he thought it was very special. On our wedding day, just as we were pronounced man and wife and turned around to face the audience, my husband saw Sarah!

He said he saw three figures dressed in soft pastels, about the age of young teenagers. They were hovering over a statue of the Blessed Virgin in the back of the church. The center girl was the clearest, and the other two were more ethereal. Her garment was a soft pink color, and she wore a gold banner that said "Sarah."

Our daughter was born nine months and one day after the day of our wedding. When she was born, I looked at her and said, "Oh, it's Sarah Marie!"

As our daughter has grown over the years, I often hear that joyous voice that connects me back to the hearing of her name years before. Sarah truly is a joyous child who relishes and loves life.

〜

Before Angelina was conceived, I remember knowing that a soul was hovering nearby. The feeling was like when you are in a room of people and you sense that someone has just walked into the room, and then you turn around and see the person. Feeling the soul around you is like a physical pressing in of someone you know is a part of you. It just won't leave you alone!

I was anxious to bring this child forth. One night I was lying in bed awake at about 11:30 p.m. in our studio apartment. Suddenly there was a knock at the door and a little voice called, "Mommy, Mommy!"

I jumped out of bed confused because we didn't have any children, and there were none living in the building. In any case, it was too late at night for a child to be out. I opened our apartment door, but no one was there.

Chills ran down my back. Then a very peaceful

presence came over me, and I realized that the little soul who had been hovering around had come to make her presence known. Shortly thereafter, our daughter was conceived.

∽

Before conception I had an inner experience of seeing my daughter in a past embodiment. She was a Tibetan monk in an orange-colored robe sitting cross-legged. (I later learned that Tibetan monks do wear orange robes and sit cross-legged to recite their chants.) After seeing this, I thought my child was going to be a boy, but she was a little girl!

She is now two years old and looks Tibetan—with a round head, dark eyes and dark skin. She also has a very self-reliant character. The first time she heard Buddhist chants at about seven months of age, she stopped what she was doing, listened and swayed back and forth. It was as if she remembered doing this from her Tibetan life.

∽

Before birth, each soul is shown her mission for that life. That mission may involve paying her debts to people she has wronged in the past, pursuing a particular profession, or bringing love and kindness into the world. The mission is very specific to each soul. And each soul can choose whether or not to fulfill that mission.

The soul is also wise. She knows the past and its application to the present and the future. And she knows what she needs to fulfill her mission in life. Thus, sometimes the soul will convey her specific needs to the pregnant mother in unique ways. The mother will often find herself intuitively drawn to things she usually has no interest in.

֍

During my second pregnancy, I devoured books about Eastern saints. I had never been particularly interested in them before. When my daughter was born, she looked Eastern, with small, fine-boned features (similar to Gandhi). From a young age, she has been very altruistic. Once she told me that she wanted to marry someone rich so she could give poor children toys.

֍

In my first pregnancy, I was possessed with cross-word puzzles. I would do them every spare moment I had while at work and right before bedtime. I had my husband buy big books of crossword puzzles for me to do. I've never had a particular interest in cross-word puzzles before or since. Now my child is eight years old. From a very early age, she was highly verbal and articulate. She has an excellent vocabulary. Maybe the crossword puzzles helped!

❧

I was literally driven to learn how to crochet during one of my pregnancies. Finding no one who would teach me, I picked up a book and taught myself. I found comfort in praying and crocheting by the hour. In addition, I really got into baking bread for our family. It was a delight to use my hands to knead the dough and prepare creative meals.

I was a bit surprised at the birth to discover that I had been carrying a baby boy. But as it turns out, this particular boy is very good with his hands. He can fix almost anything! And I have always had the feeling that all the crocheting and praying I did during that pregnancy was somehow helping his soul to heal certain karmic conditions.

❧

Karma and Reincarnation as Opportunity

Along with memories of the past, the soul carries with her the records of karma from lifetime to lifetime. *Karma* is a Sanskrit word that means "action" or "deed." The law of karma is the law of cause and effect and retribution. As the Hindu epic the Mahabharata explains, "Just as a farmer plants a certain kind of seed and gets a certain crop, so it is with good and bad deeds."[1] Or, as the Bible says, "Whatsoever a man soweth, that shall he also reap."[2]

Jesus' entire Sermon on the Mount concerns the

consequences of thoughts, feelings, words and deeds. In this sermon he gives a precise summary of the law of karma: "With the judgment you make you will be judged, and the measure you give will be the measure you get." He goes on to give the Golden Rule: "In everything do to others as you would have them do to you; for this is the law and the prophets."[3]

The karmic records of the soul include not only actions and deeds but also positive and negative patterns of thinking and feeling. Negative karmic patterns can sometimes deter a soul from making right choices, simply because of the habit of thinking or feeling in a certain way. These habits can ultimately prevent the soul from fulfilling her mission.

I see karma and reincarnation as opportunity—opportunity to learn from our mistakes on earth, to balance our debts with other souls (especially the souls within our families) and to pursue our oneness with God. And I think of earth as a schoolroom. We each have lessons to learn—like loving, forgiving and getting along with other people. If we don't graduate from earth's schoolroom in one lifetime, reincarnation gives us another chance to make amends.

With an awareness of the concept of reincarnation, we can more easily understand that the children we bear are often mature souls—sometimes more highly evolved than we ourselves. And communication with the souls of our children before and during pregnancy is one of the most rewarding experiences parents can have!

Spiritual Guides Assist the Soul Before Birth

Just as parents can help the souls of their children before birth, heaven also helps them. By hypnotic regression, psychologist Helen Wambach probed the subconscious minds of her subjects and helped them access memories of life before birth. Her book *Life Before Life* recounts many stories of people who remember pre-birth meetings with a group of spiritual guides, whom they also refer to as counselors, advisers or judges.4

The literature on near-death experiences (NDEs) tells us about the life review we can expect to go through after death. Sometimes NDEers report seeing spiritual guides in the other world. These guides gently assist the soul after each lifetime by objectively reviewing her thoughts and deeds within the larger context of her many lives. Thus the knowledge that the soul gleans from the review of the previous life enables her to prepare for the next one.

After a certain period of time in preparation for the next life, the soul meets again with spiritual guides. She discusses her assigned mission with these guides, along with all the possibilities that life may offer for that particular lifetime.

These highly advanced spiritual beings understand

the soul's karmic debts and her need for specific lessons in life. In *Life Between Life*, Joel Whitton and Joe Fisher say that in writing the life plan for the soul, or "karmic script," the recommendations of these guides are made according to what the soul needs—not necessarily what she wants.[5]

These spiritual guides also help determine when and where souls will embody. They assign souls to specific families and communities, measuring out the karma that must be balanced between groups of people and bringing together souls who have a common mission.

‿

Three months before I conceived my first child, I woke up one morning and was suddenly taken to a higher plane of awareness. I was standing in a circle with four male adults.

One stepped forward into the circle. He appeared to have a strong presence of justice and freedom about him. I realized he was the soul of my child-to-be. I became pregnant exactly three months later. I could feel his presence throughout the pregnancy.

Now, six years later, I realize that the circle of four male adults I was shown was my family-to-be. My husband and I now have three boys.

‿

The Karma and Mission of Family Members

There are a number of reasons why souls are assigned to specific families. Sometimes a child is assigned to a family because one or both parents have good karma with the soul of that child. Sometimes it's because something needs to be resolved between the parents and the child or between the child and his siblings from relationships in past lives. And sometimes it's a little of both—a little good karma and a little nonresolution.

↞

I've had children I've really welcomed back, children I knew I had been with for many lifetimes. And then I've had children who were more like strangers to me. You can definitely feel the difference.

↞

I used to know a family in Colorado in which all the family members had a common mission involving music. The father and mother played stringed instruments, and there were seven or eight children in this family. Every child, including the one-year-old, played the violin.

The reason all these children could play violin so well and at such an early age was because their souls had developed this talent in previous lives. These souls were attracted to this husband and wife and to their family because they had a group karma that was a good karma.

Sometimes the same souls in a family group evolve through changing relationships in different lives. These souls are given many opportunities to be together, either to face the challenges of negative karmic ties or to fulfill a specific purpose.

⌐

At a very early age (about three years old) my daughter, Melissa, was fascinated with my father, who had died when I was a young girl. Melissa grieved about not having met my father. She would talk about him, ask me lots of questions and want to hear stories about him.

This went on for several years. At night I would have to sit with her for half an hour to help her work through this. Sometimes she would look sad and would say to me, "You know what I'm sad about."

The night before my second child was born, Melissa had a dream. She told me that she had seen Grandpa and that they had had a big party because Grandpa was finally coming back.

The following day my son was born. Since then, Melissa has not had the same sadness and doesn't talk about Grandpa like she did before.

⌐

No matter who we are or how advanced we may be intellectually, spiritually, professionally or in any other way, we do have karma. And the more karmic debts we balance, the less likely we are to have children who come to our families because of negative karmic ties.

Chance Plays No Part in Adoption

So what about adopted children? How are they assigned to their families? And what are their karmic relationships with their biological parents and their adoptive parents?

⤿

I knew a couple who couldn't have children, so they decided to adopt a child through an agency. They were told that it would take from six months to a year to get the child. The policy of the agency was that when a child became available, the next couple on the list would be called. The couple would have a few days or even less to then go and pick up the child.

After about eight months of waiting, the husband woke up one night and said to his wife: "I know it! Our baby has been born." It was as though he had been shown the child being born. This was a man who did not typically have these kinds of experiences, yet he felt as sure as his own name that it had happened. The next morning the agency called to tell them that their baby had been born.

⤿

Most of Dr. Wambach's subjects who were adopted as children said that they had not known their biological mother or father in a past life. But they did have karmic ties with the adoptive parents.

Dr. Wambach says: "The karmic ties with the adoptive parents were most interesting. Some of them knew before they were born of the relationship they would have with the adoptive parents, and felt that they would not be able to come to them as their own genetic child but chose the method of adoption as a way to reach their parents." She concluded from her research that chance and accident apparently play no part in adoption.[6]

So the karma of one or both of the biological parents may necessitate that they give birth to a certain child so the child can get to his real parents, who may not be able to have children. And if the birth of that child is not a necessity of karma, it is a service that the biological parents can perform to enable that soul to fulfill her mission.

The following is a story of how one woman learned that there are angels who assist in the process of connecting children to their adoptive parents.

෴

My husband and I tried to have children for over ten years. We underwent many tests, procedures, in vitro fertilization and several surgeries. After the stress of all these procedures, we took a vacation from the whole fertility issue and pursued inner healing.

Several months into this healing time, I had a magnificent dream out of the blue. In this dream, I saw an image of a couple connected by an arc of light to a baby. The couple was in the top right-hand corner of the image and the baby was in the bottom left-hand area. I remember feeling as if the couple might have been in North America and the baby in South America.

This image faded and suddenly the next image appeared. It was the top half of a large, magnificent angel. Her face was profoundly compassionate and she was smiling sweetly. Her wings spanned the width of the image, in rosy pink hues. Then I noticed that above the angel was a light blue banner or scroll with ribbons on either end. It spanned the entire image and had the words "Adoption Angel" written on it.

Since then, my husband and I have started the adoption process (for Latin American, Tibetan or Indian children) and feel most confident that the adoption angel will connect us to the children God intends us to have.

∽

Regardless of whether the parents are biological or adoptive, what is important in our families is that our karma be balanced and that the rough edges of our relationships be smoothed. Karmic debts to the soul of your child can be balanced by the loving care you give to that child and by heartfelt prayer. In chapters 3 and 6, you will learn how to invoke a unique spiritual energy that can help you balance karma with the soul of your child before birth, during pregnancy and throughout his entire life.

You Can Ask God for a Soul with Specific Talents or Virtues

Many devout people who were also parents (such as the parents of Isaac, of Samuel, of Mary and of John the Baptist) prepared for their children for years and years— fasting and praying, imploring and loving God, and keeping their relationships harmonious. If they could become parents of highly evolved souls, so can you and I.

A life that is devout and consecrated to spiritual preparation for parenting becomes a magnet in your heart. And it is this magnet of love and devotion in your heart that can determine what kind of soul you will attract to your family as your child.

So whether you are contemplating your first child or are hoping to expand your family, you can pray to God and ask him to give you a soul with specific spiritual qualities. You may want to ask for a strong and honor-able soul who will be a great leader or teacher. You may ask for a child with particular talents in art, science, music or athletics. You may ask for a child with specific virtues, such as kindness, courage, selflessness or wisdom. Or you may simply ask for a happy and healthy child. But whatever you desire, ask that you might receive.

↩

When I was four to six weeks pregnant with my first child, I fell in love with a sweet angel picture of a blond-haired, blue-eyed child. I said to God, "This is what I want, a heaven-sent soul!" My child was born looking just like this angel picture. Her father has very dark hair and brown eyes, so it was quite a surprise.

↩

One day my daughter, Penelope, walked into my bedroom and said, "Mommy, I want to have a baby sister."

And I said, "Well, honey, you need to ask God first."

"OK," she said, "Let's ask him right now.

"Dear God, please put a baby in Mommy's tummy so I can have a baby sister."

Within three weeks, I conceived. It was a girl.

↩

If you are asking for a soul with exceptional talents, tell God what commitments you are willing to make for the sake of that child—for instance, giving daily prayers, seeking the best possible education, maintaining harmony in the home, and so forth. Then once you make a commitment, be sure you fulfill it.

Many parents have found it very helpful to write a letter to God when contemplating having a child. In this letter, you may include your requests and commitments. Then burn the letter, offering a prayer asking that the angels deliver it.

↜

I had a difficult time with my first pregnancy due to emotional strains and physical problems. This caused me to feel insecure. And even during the period after my baby was born, things did not go smoothly.

So when I contemplated having a second child, many of these insecurities welled up in me. I felt unworthy to be a mother to a special child. Nevertheless, I felt I was supposed to have more children, so I decided to write a letter to God about my desire to be the mother of a special child.

Then one day I was meditating in a quiet setting, and I had a very precious and unexpected experience. In my meditation, I was sitting in a church in front of a beautiful altar. There was a door to the right of the altar. It opened and an angel came through the door, holding a baby.

With the greatest care, love and gentleness pour-
ing into this baby, the angel walked over and placed
the baby in my arms. The baby was dressed in a
beautiful white christening dress.
I found out one week later that I was pregnant.

꙳

When you ask God and spiritually prepare your-
selves for an advanced soul, you will be amazed how
God responds. For example, you may be karmically
obligated to give birth to someone you injured,
neglected or even killed in a previous life. Your dedication to spiritual practices and a commitment to a greater
cause may enable you to balance your karma with that
soul many times over. Thus by the grace of God, you
may be relieved of the obligation to bear that soul and
instead be given a soul you have less karma with.

So there is a pot of gold at the end of the rainbow of
dedication. There is always a reward. But most important, whatever child God grants you, love and protect
that child as if he were the most precious child on the
planet. Accept that child for who he is, knowing that
God's great wisdom has given you the child who is right
for your family. And give praise and gratitude to God for
the priceless opportunity to assist that child in fulfilling
his purpose in life.

CHAPTER TWO

Prepare for Your Child by Healing Your Soul

You are the bows from which your children
  as living arrows are sent forth.
The archer sees the mark upon the path of
  the infinite, and He bends you with His might
  that His arrows may go swift and far.
Let your bending in the archer's hand be
  for gladness;
For even as He loves the arrow that flies, so
  He loves also the bow that is stable.

      —KAHLIL GIBRAN

When the soul returns to earth in a new body, she has locked within her the unlimited potential to fulfill her mission. However, that potential may not fully develop unless the soul has the proper environment. The life led by the child's future parents prior to conception and throughout pregnancy is a crucial factor in preparing the environment for the child.

Thus this chapter, as well as chapters 3 through 5, concentrates on spiritual preparation for parenting. In these chapters you will learn specific exercises you can do to effectively prepare yourself for conception, pregnancy and childbirth. In the final four chapters, 6 through 9, you will find out how to directly nurture and assist your baby's soul before birth.

Preparation for parenting is a time of growth and self-reflection. And it is a time for change—be it adopting a better diet, developing more compassion for others or overcoming some bad habits.

We are compelled by love to improve the quality of our lives when we contemplate the glorious mission of being a mother or father to a child. For we know that parenting exemplifies the highest love—laying down our lives for our children. You can begin your preparation for parenting by giving that highest love to your own soul.

What Is the Soul?

The soul is a popular topic today. People talk about and write about the soul. They know that the soul is important, but they may not know why.

What, then, is the soul?

And how does one love and nurture the soul?

We can think of the soul as a glistening, transparent sphere that has been evolving for a very long time. The soul is a continuum in God from the beginning. She has lived in the infinite past and she will live in the infinite future. Even though the soul is mortal, she can become immortal through oneness with her Higher Self. Your Higher Self is your individual God-identity, and it possesses all the qualities of God.[1]

The soul is highly sensitive and intuitive. At the same time, she is innocent and vulnerable, impressionable and easily led astray. She is often colored by her surroundings. She is wounded by mental and emotional toxins and by physical or verbal abuse.

Our souls urgently need our comfort and consolation, our soothing words. They need to know that we will protect them from harm. We can lovingly care for our souls as we would care for our children. Or we can neglect our souls and become the victims of our self-neglect.

Have you ever considered the possibility that in this life and/or past lives you may have neglected the development of your soul, choosing instead to develop your ego? Or that you may not have nurtured your soul—this essential "life essence" that mirrors both your personality and the personality of God? What you have drawn from these two personalities, how you have integrated the two and incorporated them into your unique soul awareness, defines your soul identity.

We Are the Parents and Teachers of Our Souls

The Book of Proverbs says, "Train up a child in the way he should go: and when he is old, he will not depart from it."[2] These words refer to one's offspring as well as to one's soul. The soul is our child until she comes of age, and so we must learn to love and protect, instruct and discipline her.

Tending the needs of your soul with sensitivity and kindness is the first step in training to be a mother or father. This is because your soul represents the child who lives inside you. Psychologists have dubbed this aspect of the soul "the inner child." And you are your soul's parent and teacher, even as you are her student.

It is your responsibility to teach your soul what is

real and of enduring worth and therefore to be kept—
and what is not real and not of enduring worth and
therefore to be laid aside. Thus, you can learn to love
your soul not only as the handiwork of God but as your
own handiwork. If you do not love what you see or what
you have made of yourself, know that God's love is
the power to change all that is not a part of your real
identity.

You can easily tell when people are happy with
themselves. They are usually joyful and self-entertained,
and they can readily laugh at themselves and their own
mistakes. They don't take themselves too seriously and
thus dive into a spiral of self-condemnation when they
make an error along the way.

Realize, then, that when you feel irritable, when you
are burdened with your circumstances, when you are
unhappy when you are alone, these are indications that
you lack inner resolution. All of these things create the
propensity to move away from God when facing the
challenges of life. And parenting certainly provides
many of those challenges.

A parent's negative patterns of thought and feeling
can create the nearly indelible impression upon a child
that he or she is bad or unworthy. And this transferal
often stems from the fact that the parents do not love
themselves in and as God.

So you may not like yourself for your mistakes or

your gruffness or anger or other negative traits, and that is understandable. But do not condemn yourself. Learn to forgive yourself and move on.

Understand Your Psychology and Heal Your Soul

Whether you are contemplating having your first child or your eighth, understanding the psychology of your soul is essential. Negative interactions between parents and children often represent areas of unresolved psychology. Sometimes these interactions are based on unresolved experiences or karmic relationships from previous lives.

The soul must learn how to work through the burdens of her unresolved karma that are reflected in the burdens of her unresolved psychology. The soul is attentive and relieved when she gets to the place where she can understand why she has repetitive negative patterns in her life that she cannot seem to correct. Many of us have experienced this.

You can begin to learn more about your psychology by identifying your positive and negative patterns of thought and feeling. But negative patterns do not go away just because you recognize them. They go away because you pray about them *and* you learn your lessons, often in the school of hard knocks. And then one day you stop beating your head against the wall and you open your eyes and you *see*, you *know*, because the mist that blocked your seeing and your knowing is cleared. And what was a mystery is no longer a mystery.

Through these learning experiences, the soul begins the process of healing and resolution. And the healing of the soul is a top priority. So every morning you can think of yourself as the good physician going forth to heal your soul. If you do all things well in your spiritual preparations for parenting but neglect the healing of your soul, your children will eventually suffer the consequences.

According to your ability to deal gently and compassionately with your own soul, so will God entrust you with a precious child. And with a keen understanding of your own soul psychology, a deep bond of love between you and your spouse and your children can be secured for a lifetime.

Your Psychology Can Affect
Your Child's Relationship to God

As you learn more and more about your psychology and seek resolution through love and forgiveness, you will find yourself forming and reforming your identity as a parent. Your identity as a parent begins with knowing that you are a representative of God to your child. And the child's first understanding of the nature of the Father-Mother God is based on his relationship with his parents.

A strong and gentle father conveys to the child that God as Father is strong and gentle. A demanding and condemning father may instill fear in the child that God is a tyrant. The same is true of the child's relationship with his mother. If the mother is sensitive and nurturing, the child experiences God as Mother in the same way. If the mother is impatient and critical, the child's concept of God may be similar and he may fear or resent God.

The memories of our relationships with our parents, residing in the subconscious or unconscious, form the foundation of our relationship to God. Thus inner wholeness with the Father-Mother God is a path that must begin with resolving our relationships with our own fathers and mothers.

When you exemplify this wholeness to your child, he feels secure that God is loving and nurturing. This sense of security allows for his spontaneous self-expression and self-discovery. And it builds a solid foundation for the development of his self-esteem and strength of character.

If you had a rough relationship with one or both of your parents, you are likely to transfer to your child, consciously or unconsciously, unresolved feelings such as resentment, distrust, anger or hatred. These suppressed feelings and negative patterns of communication from childhood have a way of resurfacing when you are faced with the challenges of parenting. And they will most likely be transmitted to your own children unless you make a conscious decision to root them out.

❧

I remember one day when two of my children, boys ages five and seven, were playing with each other. I was in another room folding clothes, and I heard the younger boy crying out for me. I had gotten used to their playful tussles so I didn't respond too quickly. But after a while, I decided to check on them.

When I went into the other room, I saw my older boy sitting on top of his younger brother. He had pinned the younger boy's arms down and would not let him up. The younger boy was in distress but was not hurt.

When I saw this scene, I felt a surge of intense emotional energy. Before I even had time to think, I quickly pulled my older son off the younger one. Both boys were as surprised as I was about my overreaction.

It was not until several months later when doing some work on my psychology that I realized where this reaction came from. I remembered seeing my father kneeling on top of my mother in the same position as my son on top of his brother. My father was physically abusive to my mother and he would pin her down in this manner and yell at her or hit her. I remembered how angry I was at my father for abusing her in this way.

Naturally I cried when I relived this memory. I hadn't thought about it for years. But it was very helpful to become aware of this memory because I was then able to have compassion for my own soul for having experienced this abusive scenario many, many times as a child. And I could forgive myself for my anger because I could see the cause as something outside of myself. This helped me to realize that I would never be completely free of these feelings until I had forgiven my parents for their abuse of each other.

Consequently, when I found myself observing this same type of scenario with my boys on a number of occasions after that first incident, I still felt anxious and upset—but I was in control. I understood where the feelings were coming from and I was able to work through the situations with my children in a more helpful manner.

 ❧

Healing Through Forgiveness

One important key in resolving your relationships with your parents is forgiveness. Do you love enough to forgive the wrongdoings of your parents? Do you forgive yourself for any psychological problems you have as a result of the hurts, misunderstandings, guilt, anger or pain of growing up?

When you forgive yourself and your parents, you begin to take accountability for your problems. And when you take this level of accountability, you begin the healing process. Sidney and Suzanne Simon in their book *Forgiveness: How to Make Peace with Your Past and Get On with Your Life* explain that healing is an ongoing process that requires hard work:

> Inner peace is found by changing yourself, *not* the people who hurt you. And you change your-self *for yourself*, for the joy, serenity, peace of mind, understanding, compassion, laughter, and bright future that you get. These are the rewards *you* can receive. The people you forgive benefit, too—but that is not why you forgive them.
>
> However, make no mistake about it, you will have to work for these things. You will have to work long and hard to heal your wounds and make peace with your past. There are no short cuts, no ways around the fact that *forgiveness is possible if and only if you commit yourself to an ongoing healing process.*[3]

Forgiveness begins with understanding that you *and* your parents are imperfect. You make mistakes and they make mistakes. But that doesn't mean that you are bad people or that you can't love one another. You can heal your own soul by extending to others what you would like them to extend to you: love and forgiveness. And you can give the following affirmation for forgiveness of yourself and others.

I AM* forgiveness acting here,
Casting out all doubt and fear,
Setting men forever free
With wings of cosmic victory.

I AM calling in full power
For forgiveness every hour;
To all life in every place
I flood forth forgiving grace.

You Are Loved Perfectly by the Father-Mother God

As you pursue forgiveness and healing in preparation for parenting, take periods of time alone to meditate on your heart and soul. Realize that in the beginning God made you in his image, and you were conceived in the love of the Father-Mother God. It was the perfect love of God as Father and God as Mother for each other out of which you were born and out of which you became a unique manifestation of love.

I truly believe that the point of alienation from

*See page 51 for an explanation of the esoteric meaning of "I AM."

reality is that point where we feel that we are not loved perfectly by our Father-Mother God—especially as we have experienced the burdens of our relationships with our human fathers and mothers.

At this very moment you are being re-created out of the love of the Father-Mother God. That love perpetually burns on the altar of your heart as a spiritual flame. That flame in your heart is the spark of your divinity and it sustains your life. The light of God flows from your Higher Self into your heart flame moment by moment. The heart flame is your point of contact with God and with your incoming child.

THE HEART FLAME

There is no greater comfort in the universe than to know that you are a child loved by the Father-Mother God. As you receive this comfort in your heart, you can impart it as the greatest gift to your child from conception to birth and beyond.

Two Special Friends in Heaven to Assist You

Another great comfort for many expectant parents has come from the intercession of two special friends in heaven: Kuan Yin, the Eastern bodhisattva and Mother of Mercy, and Mary, the mother of Jesus. These two representatives of God as Mother can assist you in any area of your life, including the healing of your soul and overcoming difficulties in conceiving or problems during pregnancy.

Kuan Yin is the saviouress whose beauty, grace and compassion have come to represent the ideal of womanhood in the East. A great white veil covers her entire form and she may be seated on a lotus.

Kuan Yin is often portrayed with a child in her arms, near her feet or on her knees, or with several children around her. Those who wish to have children customarily seek her assistance, since she is widely regarded as the bestower of children. She is the patron saint of families and of childbearing. You can have no greater ally than Kuan Yin.

⌒

One night I was playing a Chinese music tape dedicated to Kuan Yin. I remember falling into a deep sleep and seeing Kuan Yin bring a baby to me. I knew immediately this baby had been a Buddhist monk in a previous life. The baby's energy was so strong I could feel it swooshing around me. I also heard the baby's voice talking to me. The voice was calm and melodic.

One day my oldest daughter, Jennifer, walked up to me and said, "You are going to have a girl and her name is Anna." When I asked her how she knew, Jennifer replied, "She was my daughter a long, long time ago, when we were Buddhists." A sonogram later revealed the baby was a girl, and we began calling her Anna.

During labor I played musical mantras to Kuan Yin. It was the most peaceful birth I have ever experienced! Upon delivery of my baby the nurse remarked, "She looks like she is smiling." To this day, I know Kuan Yin has blessed our family with the gift of a peaceful Buddhist monk.

⮌

The Blessed Virgin Mary, the mother of Jesus, is traditionally regarded as the Queen of Angels. She is very close to people on earth even today, as evidenced by her many appearances around the planet. Although she is traditionally revered primarily by Catholics, any of us can claim her as our mother, our sister, our teacher and our friend.

We give our adoration to Mary through the giving of the rosary. When you give the rosary to Mary, she can transfer her light and attainment to you for holding the vision of the highest good for you and your unborn child.

The new-age "Hail Mary" at the end of this chapter

invokes her presence with us in the hour when we need her most. The words of this "Hail Mary" differ slightly from the traditional version, which affirms we are sinners. I believe that God does not want us to see ourselves as sinners. Rather, we can affirm our identity as sons and daughters of God and ask Mary to pray for our victory over sin, disease and death.

You can also ask Mary to place her immaculate heart over your heart to help solve any problems in your life. Many people believe they have experienced healing through her intercession.

~

Prior to my pregnancy, I felt a strong desire to have children. For three months, I saw the Blessed Virgin handing me a beautiful baby.

Eventually I got pregnant. During my first trimester, I often gave the rosary and mantras to Kuan Yin.[4] I also meditated on a picture of the immaculate heart of Mary and a Kuan Yin statue I had.

I entered my fourth month of pregnancy and my body threatened miscarriage. My law books weighed fifty pounds and I walked up a very steep hill to classes. I began to have heavy spotting. My body was undergoing too much physical stress. I called my doctor, who saw me immediately. The doctor did not give me much hope. She sent me home to rest and to wait.

I was determined not to lose this baby.

I remember driving home and repeatedly saying the Hail Mary. I put on a rosary cassette tape and played it constantly.⁵ Throughout the day and night, I meditated on Mary and recited her mantra. I would wake up talking to the baby and telling her how much I loved her and wanted her to stay. With the loving help of the Virgin Mary, the baby and I passed our crisis and the threat of miscarriage. I gave birth to a beautiful girl.

These two representatives of God as Mother can assist you in any area of your life if you ask them to. Pray for their intercession, meditate on their images and recite their mantras.

Kuan Yin

Om Mani Padme Hum
(Hail to the jewel in the lotus)

Na-Mo Sung Tzu Kuan Yin
(Homage to Kuan Yin, the bestower of children)

MARY

Hail, Mary, full of grace!
The Lord is with thee.
Blessed art thou among women
And blessed is the fruit of thy womb, Jesus.

Holy Mary, Mother of God,
Pray for us, sons and daughters of God,
Now and at the hour of our victory
Over sin, disease and death.

CHAPTER THREE

A Unique
Spiritual Energy
for Healing
and Transformation

I rescue all who cling to me,

I protect whoever knows my name,

I answer everyone who invokes me.

—PSALM 91:14, 15

One of the most effective spiritual ways to heal your-self and assist your unborn baby comes from an unexpected source—the creative power of sound. Recent scientific studies confirm what sages have known for thousands of years: sound can create matter and it can change matter. And it can create spiritual and material changes in our lives.

We know that sound can be a dramatic destructive force. A high-pitched note can shatter a wineglass. A sonic boom can crack plaster. A gunshot can trigger an avalanche. But sound can also be used constructively. Doctors and health practitioners use ultrasound for everything from cleaning wounds to diagnosing tumors. Some alternative medical practitioners are experiment-ing with using specific tones to heal organs. And some researchers are looking at the effects of prayer and chanting on human health and well-being.

The Transforming Effect of Sound

A group of Benedictine monks discovered an unex-pected benefit from their use of sound in giving Grego-rian chants: chanting seemed to energize them. For hundreds of years the monks of the Benedictine order had kept a rigorous schedule, sleeping only a few hours a night and chanting from six to eight hours a day. When a new abbot changed the schedule and cut out the chanting, the monks became tired and lethargic. The more sleep they got, the more tired they seemed to become.

In 1967 Alfred Tomatis, a French physician, psychologist and ear specialist, was called in to find out what was wrong with them. He found that the monks had, in fact, been "chanting in order to 'charge' themselves."[1] He reintroduced chanting, along with a program of listening to stimulating sounds, and the monks soon found the energy to return to their normal schedule.

For centuries, Hindus and Buddhists have used mantras in their devotions and observed their effects. A mantra is a word or combination of words held to be sacred. Many mantras are composed of Sanskrit words. According to Hindu tradition, mantras were received as divine inspiration by mystics who were able to hear the fundamental tones of the universe.

Hindu writings tell us that yogis have used mantras along with visualizations to light fires, materialize food and other physical objects, bring rain, and even influence the outcome of battles. But producing physical change wasn't the primary goal of the yogis. They used mantras primarily to gain protection, wisdom, enhanced concentration, enlightenment and oneness with God.

Some of the best examples of the transforming effect of sound come from the Bible. When the Israelites "shouted with a great shout," the walls of Jericho came tumbling down. At Jesus' command, the sick were healed and evil spirits fled. And the man lame from birth walked for the first time when Peter commanded, "In the name of Jesus Christ of Nazareth, rise up and walk!"[2]

The sound that can transform our spiritual and material worlds isn't just any sound. It's the Word of God. In the ancient Hindu Vedas we read, "In the beginning was Brahman with whom was the Word, and the Word is Brahman."[3] Similarly, the apostle John wrote, "In the beginning was the Word, and the Word was with God, and the Word was God." And Genesis says that when God *spoke* the words "Let there be light," the process of creation began.[4]

Spoken Prayer Is More Effective Than Silent Prayer

Hindus and Buddhists aren't the only ones who use the power of the Word. Prayers are spoken, sung and chanted in churches, temples and mosques around the world. Christians pray the Our Father or the Hail Mary. Jews give the Shema and Muslims the Shahadah. Perhaps the practice is so widespread because people of many religions instinctively recognize the effectiveness of spoken prayer.

No matter what religion you practice (or none), you can harness the creative power of the Word of God through spoken prayer. There are different forms of spoken prayer such as chants, mantras and affirmations. But as many people have discovered, the form called decrees is the most effective for change—for you and for your unborn baby. Like prayers, decrees are spoken petitions to God. But more than that, they are a worded formula, a command for the will of God to manifest.

〜

When I first heard about decrees, I couldn't understand why I had to give them out loud. I was by nature inclined to silence and meditation. Decrees seemed like silly verses to me.

A persistent friend encouraged me to use them, so one day I decided to give them another try. I said a silent prayer: "God, explain to me why I should do this. If there's any value and positive action in decrees, show me!" And I began to give the decree "I AM the violet flame . . ." [page 130].

I felt myself lifted into another realm of consciousness. An intense pink-white light enveloped me, and from behind I heard the rushing of powerful wings approaching at great speed. Somehow I knew that it was an angel.

Then I realized I was still giving the decree. I saw how the words of the decree were changed into energy that in turn formed into a large sphere of glowing white light right in front of my mouth. The moment the sphere formed, two beautiful hands plucked it from my lips and disappeared with it at lightning speed. Then the vision faded.

It all happened in a split second. The light around me subsided and I floated back into my normal consciousness. I don't know who the angel was, but I was left with a vivid understanding of what happens when we give decrees. I've given them ever since.

⤳

Using the Name of God in Decrees

One of the reasons decrees are such an effective form of prayer is that they include the name of God. When God spoke to Moses out of the burning bush, he revealed that his name is I AM THAT I AM.[5] Decrees often simply use "I AM" rather than the full name. So, when we say "I AM," what we are really saying is "God in me is. . . ." Thus we affirm our oneness with God and access his infinite love, wisdom and power.

Whatever you say following the words "I AM" will become a reality in your world, for the light of God flowing through you will make it so. This is the deeper meaning of the so-called mind-body connection. The state of your body *is* influenced by what you think—and by what you say. Your words are a self-fulfilling prophecy. So if you catch yourself saying, "I am tired" or "I am just not good enough," stop and redirect the power of God within you by saying, "In the name of God I AM THAT I AM and according to God's will, I AM full of energy" or "I AM worthy."

When you use the name of God, you enlist the discriminating intelligence of your Higher Self to make certain that only the will of God is manifest through your decrees. Your decrees will then produce change within your heart, body, mind and soul at all levels and retroactively through all past lifetimes since you departed from the perfection of God.

The Violet Fire: A Unique Spiritual Energy

You can use the decrees and mantras throughout this book to command the flow of God's energy into your life as you prepare for parenting. Through decrees you can also invoke a unique spiritual energy called the violet fire.

The violet fire, also called the violet flame, can create all sorts of positive change in you. It can heal physical problems and increase your stamina. It can also help transform unresolved psychological problems in your subconscious mind that might otherwise take years of therapy to resolve.

The violet flame is the joie de vivre that can lift your spirits, and it is the flame of forgiveness. It can help you get through unresolved past experiences with your parents or other people in your life who have wronged you or whom you have wronged.

The violet flame can also transmute negative karma from this and previous lifetimes. To *transmute* means to alter in form, appearance or nature, especially to change something into a higher form. The term was used by alchemists who attempted to transmute base metals into gold, separating the "subtle" from the "gross" by means of heat. For both ancient and medieval alchemists, the real purpose of alchemical transmutation was spiritual transformation and the attainment of eternal life.

That is precisely what the violet flame can do for you. It can consume elements of your karma so that you can realize the true gold of your Higher Self.

While we have done much good in our lifetimes, we have also created negative energy that has collected and then calcified in our physical, mental and emotional worlds. As a result, we don't feel as light, free, happy, vibrant and spiritual as we could. The violet flame can consume the debris within and between the atoms of your being.

When you invoke the violet flame, this is how it works. It envelops each atom individually. Instantaneously a polarity is set up between the nucleus of the atom and the white light in the core of the flame. The nucleus, being matter, assumes the negative pole. And the light of the violet flame, being Spirit, assumes the positive pole.

The interaction between the nucleus of the atom and the light in the violet flame establishes an oscillation. This oscillation dislodges the densities that are trapped between the electrons orbiting the nucleus. As this substance is loosened, the electrons begin to move more freely and the debris is thrown into the violet flame.

This action takes place at nonphysical, or "metaphysical," dimensions of matter. On contact with the violet flame, the dense substance is transmuted, restored to its native purity and returned to your Higher Self.

The way to invoke the violet flame is by reciting the violet-flame mantras at the end of this chapter or those at the end of chapter 6. You can experiment with giving these decrees for transmutation, healing and spiritual transformation. For instance, give five to fifteen minutes of violet-flame decrees each day, then notice the changes you experience after a week or a month.

Repetition and Visualization Enhance Decrees

You will receive greater benefit from your violet-flame decrees if you repeat each decree a number of times. In the East, people repeat their mantras over and over, even thousands of times a day. But in the West we are less accustomed to the idea of repeating a prayer.

People often say, "Why should I have to ask God for something more than once?" But repeating a decree or mantra is not simply making the same request over and over. Each time you repeat a decree, you are increasing its effectiveness.

Every moment God's energy is flowing to you from your Higher Self. So while you are giving your mantras and decrees, you are continuously charging all this energy with God's light. The more you decree, the more positive energy you acquire and the more you can send out into the world to bless others.

Imagine you are sitting next to a stream and you pour a gallon of purple dye into it. The water in front of you turns a deep purple, but the purple water flows downstream and soon the water in front of you is clear again. If you want to color the entire stream purple, you have to keep pouring gallons of purple dye into it.

It's the same way with spoken prayer. If you decree aloud for just a few minutes, your prayers will affect a situation. But a serious situation may need ongoing attention. Saying a prayer, mantra or decree once is not always enough to overcome major problems.

What you think about while you are decreeing also makes a difference in how powerful and effective your decrees are. A person who is focusing on his decrees can accomplish more in five minutes than someone who decrees all day without concentrating.

When you decree, create a mental image or visualization. You can start by closing your eyes and focusing on the flame of God in your heart or on your Higher Self, which you can see as a blazing sun of light overhead. Or you can let the words of the decree direct your visualizations. In chapters 6, 7 and 8 you will learn specific visualizations you can use during pregnancy for the healthy development of your baby.

If your attention is riveted on a specific image as you decree, the results will be infinitely more effective than if your mind wanders and you look randomly around the room. If you become distracted, gently return your mind to your focus.

The more you practice, the more skilled you will become at focusing your attention. Once you have memorized a decree, you can close your eyes as you repeat the decree and strengthen your concentration on the image you have created.

When and Where to Decree

Each morning an angel brings us our karma for the day. As soon as we wake up, that package of negative karma is waiting for us. So you can do one of two things when you wake up in the morning. You can say: "Well, I'm too busy to say my prayers right now. I'll just have to deal with this bag of karma later." If you do that, you'll probably find that your karma weighs you down all day long. Or you can get up and give your prayers and decrees first thing, and you will undoubtedly have a much smoother day.

Since spoken prayer is more effective than silent prayer, it is best to give your decrees out loud. If you can't decree aloud—because you're in a public place, for instance—you can repeat the decrees in your mind. You can give decrees anywhere, even while you're doing chores, going for a walk or driving. But try to spend at least some time each day decreeing without interruption in a quiet place.

When you are ready to decree, first give a prayer specifically naming what you want God to do for you. Then choose a decree. Speak the words with devotion and feeling. Endow each word with love for God, holding in mind your chosen visualization.

Don't be disappointed if your decrees don't seem to bring results right away or in the way you expected. Have faith that God will answer you in the way that is best for your soul and the soul of your child.

Purify Your Chakras

Many parents often intuitively feel the need for purification in order to prepare for conception. They may begin eating a healthier diet or fasting once a week to cleanse their bodies.

The process of purification before conception is important because it can increase your ability to transfer light to your child. The violet flame can tremendously assist in this process. You can invoke it and specifically ask for the purification of your memories and thoughts, your feelings and desires, and your physical body. And you can use it to purify your chakras, the spiritual centers in your body.[6]

Chakra is a Sanskrit word meaning "wheel" or "disc." Each chakra has a unique function and frequency and represents a different quality of God's consciousness. These differences are denoted by the color and the number of "petals" of each chakra. The more petals a chakra has, the higher its frequency. And the more energy that flows through a chakra, the faster it spins.

There are seven major chakras: the crown, third eye, throat, heart, solar plexus, seat of the soul, and base of the spine. Situated along the spinal column, they are invisible to the physical eye, yet your life and spiritual progress depend on their vitality.

Your chakras are receiving and sending stations for the energy of God that flows to and from you each day. They act as transformers of spiritual light, invigorating your memory, your mind, your feelings and desires, and the cells and organs of your physical body.

Unfortunately, by our interactions with others

THE SEVEN CHAKRAS OF LIGHT

CHAKRA	COLOR # PETALS	QUALITIES	RELATED ORGANS
crown	yellow 972	wisdom, calmness, fidelity	cerebrum, pituitary gland, hypothalamus
third eye	emerald green 96	vision, truth, healing	brain stem, cerebellum, pineal gland, eyes, ears
throat	sapphire blue 16	faith, power, will, strength	lungs, thyroid, larynx, trachea, vocal cords
heart	rose pink 12	love, compassion, kindness	heart, thymus, lymphatic system, diaphragm
solar plexus	purple and gold 10	peace, service, brotherhood	stomach, kidneys, pancreas, liver, gallbladder
seat of the soul	violet 6	freedom, forgiveness, joy	spleen, ovaries, testes, intestines, appendix
base of the spine	white 4	purity, discipline, order	bladder, rectum, reproductive organs

throughout our many lifetimes, karmic debris has accumulated around our chakras. This debris is like the leaves that clog a drain after it rains. In order for water to run through the drain properly, we need to clear away the leaves. Similarly, in order for God's light to flow through your chakras, you need to clear the debris that clings to those sacred centers. When your chakras are clogged, you may feel sluggish, pessimistic or sick without knowing why. When your chakras and the circuits of energy that connect them are clear, you feel more energetic, positive, joyful and giving. And when the pregnant mother's chakras are cleared, the unborn baby receives the benefit of the light of God that flows through them.

Through meditation on God and the expansion of love in your heart, the light of the Divine Mother, called the Kundalini in Eastern tradition, will rise from the base-of-the-spine chakra and activate the energies of each chakra. As this energy rises, each chakra in turn begins to spin. It opens and raises its petals, signifying the unfoldment of your latent spiritual powers.

Many people have used the violet flame to effectively clear their chakras. You can give the Violet-Fire Chakra Meditation on the following pages to purify your chakras. Each person requires a different amount of time to see tangible results, but the violet flame begins to work as soon as you invoke it. If you keep giving your violet-flame decrees, you will begin to see and feel the difference. The violet flame works miracles. You can expect one!

EXERCISE AND VISUALIZATION:

We begin our meditation with the heart chakra because it is the most important chakra. Spiritual light from your Higher Self flows into your heart chakra. From the heart chakra, this light is distributed to the other six chakras. And from the chakras, the light is distributed to all the organs, cells and nerve centers in your body.

After meditating on the heart chakra, we focus on the chakras above and below the heart in the order listed in the following violet-fire mantras. As you give these mantras, see the violet flame bathing and cleansing your chakras, dissolving the debris that has collected around them.

PREAMBLE:

You can begin this chakra meditation with the following preamble.

> In the name of God I AM THAT I AM,
> I call for the purification of my chakras.
> According to God's will, I decree:

VIOLET-FIRE CHAKRA MEDITATION

MANTRAS:

I AM a being of violet fire!
I AM the purity God desires!*

 My heart is a chakra of violet fire,
My heart is the purity God desires!

I AM a being of violet fire!
I AM the purity God desires!

 My throat chakra is a wheel of violet fire,
My throat chakra is the purity God desires!

I AM a being of violet fire!
I AM the purity God desires!

 My solar plexus is a sun of violet fire,
My solar plexus is the purity God desires!

I AM a being of violet fire!
I AM the purity God desires!

(mantras continue)

---

*For greater effectiveness, give each two-line mantra three
times or more.

mantras (continued):

My third eye is a center of violet fire,
My third eye is the purity God desires!

I AM a being of violet fire!
I AM the purity God desires!

My soul chakra is a sphere of violet fire,
My soul is the purity God desires!

I AM a being of violet fire!
I AM the purity God desires!

My crown chakra is a lotus of violet fire,
My crown chakra is the purity God desires!

I AM a being of violet fire!
I AM the purity God desires!

My base chakra is a fount of violet fire,
My base chakra is the purity God desires!

CHAPTER FOUR

How to Spiritualize Marriage and Conception

When sexual union is for the sake of heaven, there is nothing as holy or pure. The union of man and woman, when it is right, is the secret of civilization. Thereby, one becomes a partner with God in the act of Creation.

—IGGERET HA-QODESH

God has blessed the human institution of marriage as an opportunity for two individuals to develop wholeness. Marriage is meant to be mystical, commemorating the soul's reunion with God, and fruitful, blessing the earth with a magnanimous love. That love is a magnet that enables you to become more of God.

So you see the hallowed circle of marriage as a place where you love more of God and draw down more of his energy. Therefore you have a greater ability to fulfill your mission, to help others and to pay your karmic debts (especially through the intimacy of family relationships).

In the marriage relationship, as in all relationships, we are putting on more of God's consciousness by understanding one another and becoming that which we perceive of God in each other. Without relationships, we could not develop. If you put a newborn baby in a room alone and deprived him of contact with people, he would not develop. In fact, he would probably die. He needs the stimulation of other people, which is really interaction with the presence of God in each other.

So the marriage relationship is also an opportunity for spiritual development. And when you run into the inevitable challenges of marriage, you may be tempted to give up on the relationship unless you understand what a great opportunity marriage is for inner resolution and the balancing of karma.

Carrying Each Other's Karma

The meaning of man and woman being "one flesh," as the Bible says,[1] is that a man and a woman agree to carry each other's karma when they enter into the marriage contract. The marriage vow means we will carry one another's karma and we will share one another's levels of spiritual attainment.

Usually it's the attainment of the partner that stands out in the courtship relationship. We see everything that is good and beautiful and wonderful about our prospective marriage partner. Once the marriage vows have been taken, all of that remains—but the burden of the karma is also shared.

Now, most people don't know what they're getting into when they go before the altar to be married. So they take the marriage vows and they are pronounced man and wife. Then all of a sudden they wake up one morning and, as we say, "the honeymoon is over"—and they find that they have an extra pack on their back. The wife is carrying the husband's karma, and the husband is carrying the wife's karma.

Well, it's kind of like putting on someone else's

shoes. They're not quite comfortable, they're not quite worn in the right places and they don't even fit. And so all of a sudden, we start resenting this extra burden that we have taken on in this marriage relationship.

When you take the vow "for better or for worse, for richer or for poorer, in sickness and in health," you are taking a vow to share your karma. Now it becomes a joint load. The weaknesses of your spouse can be balanced by your strengths. Your own weaknesses can be balanced by your spouse's strengths. That's what marriage is for.

So as karmic cycles unfold and there is sickness or hardship, you realize this is what you have agreed to share. You may have experienced the beauties and the joys of marriage, but you must also share the unwinding of karma as it comes to you throughout life. It can be shared in bliss and transformed, especially if you invoke the violet flame.

Thus we have a choice: we can allow our karma to take over our lives and burden the marriage or we can change it. When you understand that your karma can blind you to the virtues of your partner, you can make a deliberate choice to transmute that karma and to spiritualize your marriage.

Having Realistic Expectations

We must not expect a marriage to supply the answers to all of life's problems. We might wish that somehow all the pain and sorrow of life will be eliminated and all of our greatest longings—including our dreams, fantasies and subconscious desires—will suddenly be fulfilled. But this is not the case. It is one of those illusions that society portrays.

And so we put unrealistic demands and strains upon our marriage partner. The wife expects all of these fulfillments in the husband, the husband expects all of these fulfillments in the wife—and the gods themselves could not possibly live up to all the ideals that we have concerning the supreme bliss of the married state. These demands stretch marriages to the breaking point because the partners are demanding what marriage is not intended to give.

So we need to define marriage and see what it is capable of giving and what we are capable of giving to it. We need to have a healthy, practical, down-to-earth awareness of what must take place in marriage.

Different Roles in Marriage

The way a marriage will work best is if the husband and wife understand that the marriage can contain the totality of God and the totality of human relationships. Thus there cannot be rigid roles in a fulfilling marriage relationship.

In other words, the wife is not always wife—she is every aspect of the feminine nature of God at one time or another. And so she may be mother or daughter or sister or wife. She may be child or she may be the mature matriarch—the patroness of life.

At the same time, the husband cannot play the rigid role of husband because God is not the rigid role of husband. God appears to us as father, as son, as the aspect of the Holy Spirit, as brother, as neighbor, as friend, as partner on the way—and all of these relationships can be fulfilled and they change from moment to moment.

If we are always demanding that our spouse be the epitome of our concept of what a husband is or what a wife is, we're going to be sadly disappointed because no one is rigidly one role or one person. And if we make our relationship rigid based on what society tells us marriage should be, we lose out on the richness and the depth that God has given us to experience.

These different roles give an expansive nature to the marriage relationship. We can enjoy one another as friends, as confidants, as partners in a joint endeavor or as parents of a child. We can enjoy each other in almost any capacity.

I remember counseling a woman a long time ago who could not get along with her husband. And I said, "Don't you understand that all of us at some time need a mother and we all need to provide that role? Sometimes you have to be mother even to your husband and sometimes he has to be father to you." Well, to her this was outrageous! She absolutely was not going to accept the role of mother in relation to her husband.

When this happens we miss a very important point. Somewhere deep, deep down in the soul we are all little children and there's that tender spot that still can be hurt and still reacts as a child. And we identify that in ourselves and we understand it. But when we look at someone else, we cancel it out. We say: "No, he's an adult. He should behave like an adult. He shouldn't be making demands on me that a child would make on a parent."

We lose a great opportunity when we deny any adult the right to be a child at times. Everyone has the right to be a child. Everyone has the right to be a student. And you all have moments when you are teachers without question. There is always someone who can learn from you.

So, marriage is like two intertwining flames. When you look into a physical fire, you see that you can never capture the flame and say, "This is the shape of the flame." It never has a shape—it keeps moving. The two flames in a marriage are constantly leaping, moving and taking on different characteristics of God.

And if they are two flames, they ought to be blending in harmony. When one takes a shape, the other molds itself around that shape. This is the day-to-day creativity and flow of the love that can exist between husband and wife.

Adoration of God in Your Marriage Partner

To love God in your husband or your wife is the spiritualization of marriage. To adore and worship the flame of God in your spouse is not disrespectful to God. It is to exalt the highest and the most noble in each other.

But in order to see God in each other, you must have mutual respect. And of course, to have mutual respect you must have self-respect. If you don't respect the flame of God in your own heart, you will never respect it in anyone else. If you don't love yourself first as the creation of God, you will never be able to love anyone else to his or her satisfaction or to your own.

You can love God in man or in woman and still experience physical attraction. When you come right down to it, the understanding that you are loving God in your spouse does not deprive you of anything. It simply means that all of your energies, including sexual energies, are spiritualized and that you experience love at the level of the divine union.

So how do we reconcile sexual desire with this exalted experience? Sexual desire is the desire of God to bring forth the highest creativity in every aspect of life. It is the tremendous momentum of God desiring to be in physical manifestation, and it is the momentum of energy that is needed for the union of the seed and the egg.

God did not create the universe without desire. He had to desire to have his universe. Likewise, in order for you to create—and this applies to any project or creation that you're undertaking—you must also have desire.

If you don't bring the fullness of your manhood or your womanhood into the momentum of desire, it's like a tiny little wave breaking on the shore—it just goes plunk because there's no desire behind it. But look at the marvelous bounding waves that are the big breakers, and you understand the sense of desire you must have to build your life, to become a son or daughter of God and to be an effective parent. You have to have so much desire that when the wave breaks on the shore of your life, it releases that much energy for creation.

Therefore when sexual desire is understood, the spiritualization of procreation can become the common experience of all men and women in this age—and it can be so in the twinkling of an eye. The main requirement is simply a change in consciousness. And you can be free from the prisonhouse of guilt, shame and confusion regarding sex.

No Such Thing as Original Sin

So what about sex and original sin?

The doctrine of original sin, which is still taught today, holds that as a result of the fall of Adam and Eve, every member of the human race is born with a moral defect. Even though most of us reject this doctrine in our conscious minds, we may still carry around a sense of condemnation concerning sex at subconscious levels.

When I first learned about this doctrine as a child, I could not for the life of me understand how the sins of someone who had lived five thousand or more years ago could make me a sinner. I could never understand this teaching, and I don't believe it to this day.

There's barely a trace of the concept of original sin among the early apostolic fathers. It wasn't until the fifth century that the controversy over the doctrine of original sin erupted. Saint Augustine taught that the stain of original sin was transmitted from generation to generation by the sexual act itself. And because he thought the sexual act was always accompanied by lust, he declared it inherently sinful.

There is no such thing as original sin because our origin is in God. It's that simple. Therefore, we can ask God to help us root out of our subconscious any lingering sense of impurity or condemnation about sex and procreation.

Uplifting Your Consciousness for Conception

Your thoughts and feelings at the moment of conception can be a determining factor in the kind of soul you will attract as your child. One thing you can do to uplift your consciousness, even before you are attempting to conceive, is to fill your home with spiritual music. Playing

Christmas carols (no matter what time of year) is one of the best ways to permeate your home with a sense of holiness.

It is important to choose your music carefully and learn to discern the consciousness of those who are singing. Listen for recordings by people who have angelic voices or a deep devotion (such as Mario Lanza), as these songs are intended to draw into your home the angels themselves.

My late husband Mark Prophet and I wrote the following poem as a dedication to the immaculate, or pure, conception. You can recite it to restore your own sense of purity and worthiness to be the instrument of God for the holy conception of your child. It also affirms the sacredness of life and reverence for the spark of divine love and the flow of the seed of identity from father to mother.

> Life in heaven and on earth
> Is sacred still;
> Life, the spirit of God, his worth,
> Does work His will.
>
> Where'er the radiance of his flame
> Does kindle spark,
> Cosmic arrow's aim
> Heightens perfection's mark.

Spirit endows creative love
   To sweetly flow—
No thought the image mar above
   Nor here below.

For life's sacred bark
   Sails on forever free,
And none shall break the arc
   Of our blest liberty.

You can think of your consciousness as an arrow that you shoot high into the cosmos in the moment of uniting with God in one another during sexual union. The perfection of the mark is heightened by the aim of that cosmic arrow. And that aim is the thrust of your love and your desire, of God's desire within you, to see your arrow reach the highest star—the soul of your child-to-be.

⌒

When our son was conceived, I experienced a spiritual blessing that was very special. My husband and I began our lovemaking with a simple prayer to the Blessed Virgin and the angels to consecrate our union. I felt great love in my heart for my husband and the child that I knew was to come. I had waited for many years for our union and I was filled with great joy.

As we came together, I closed my eyes and felt

our consciousness ascending in a shaft of light. We were effortlessly drawn into a high place that opened into a wide-open place of great light. I remember feeling the vastness of a golden-white light in this seemingly unending place. It was beautiful and infinitely peaceful. I did not know the meaning of the experience but felt that something special had occurred. Two weeks later I found out that I was pregnant.

⤶

Before I met my husband, he had a vision in the Himalayas of a soul who wanted to be born to him one day. And so it was that after many years of preparing to have our first child we journeyed to the Himalayas, to the source of the Ganges, to a place far removed from civilization where we could meditate and pray and commune with this soul we wanted to give birth to.

We both spent an entire day on our own doing our own spiritual practices and then came together at night. It was very special. After that, I felt like I was guarding and tending a highly valuable secret as we descended from the mountains to the plains again.

⤶

The goal of your meditation for conception is to be transported to the heights of spiritual attunement. I have selected a number of songs and decrees for meditation that can give you this level of attunement (see the Meditation for Conception on the following pages). You can give part or all of this meditation as a ritual before sexual union each time you attempt to con-ceive. Or you can select other songs, decrees, prayers or mantras that enable you to best commune with God and with the soul of your child. The playing of spiritual music gives most people a high level of attunement.

Meditation for Conception

This is a recommended meditation for those who are familiar with the Christian tradition. Begin by listening to the following songs on audiocassette or CD. Or if you know the melodies, you and your spouse may sing them together without a recording. As you sing or listen to the Lord's Prayer, focus your attention on God as Father. And for the Ave Maria, you can meditate on God as Mother.

SONG:

The Lord's Prayer

Our Father, which art in heaven
Hallowed be thy name.
Thy kingdom come
Thy will be done in earth
As it is in heaven.

Give us this day our daily bread
And forgive us our debts
As we forgive our debtors.

And lead us not into temptation
But deliver us from evil
For thine is the kingdom
And the power, and the glory, for ever.
Amen.

Melody: "The Lord's Prayer" by Albert Hay Malotte

Meditation for Conception

Ave Maria

Being of sanctity
Flower of immortality
Revered thy flame of consecration
O Mary, hallow'd is thy name
Your soul a symphony, holy and pure
    to the Christ in man.
O Father, bless her for her faith in thee
Expand her holy mantle of Light
Inspire the great, magnificent concept
The image lovely, so gentle and mild
Born of Divinity.

Holy Madonna
Pure in soul and mind
We bow to the Light you bore the earth
The Christ who enters each heart to raise
All to love, the goal of self-mastery—
    the path of great worth.
Dear Mary, we invoke thy blessed rays
Of healing power that flows from your heart
O Raphael, consecrate our pathway
And help us cosmic grace impart
Light, teach us all thou art!

(song continues)

Melody: "Ave Maria," op. 52 no. 6, by Franz Schubert

song (continued):

Blest Queen of Heaven
Great art thou!
Instruct and bless our youth and children
Enfold them with thy Presence now
Restore the mem'ry of their holy vows
    from the inner planes.
O Mother of the World, we are thy flames
Our holy God-design we claim
Rejoice, rejoice, O heavenly powers
For earth does seek thee, the God Star our aim
Victory in God's name.

Meditation for Conception

SCRIPTURAL READINGS:

The Annunciation

And in the sixth month the angel Gabriel was sent from God unto a city of Galilee named Nazareth, to a virgin espoused to a man whose name was Joseph, of the house of David, and the virgin's name was Mary.

And the angel came in unto her and said, "Hail, thou that art highly favoured, the Lord is with thee: blessed art thou among women."

And when she saw him, she was troubled at his saying and cast in her mind what manner of salutation this should be. And the angel said unto her:

"Fear not, Mary; for thou hast found favour with God. And, behold, thou shalt conceive in thy womb and bring forth a son and shalt call his name Jesus.

"He shall be great and shall be called the Son of the Highest: and the Lord God shall give unto him the throne of his father David. And he shall reign over the house of Jacob for ever, and of his kingdom there shall be no end."

Then said Mary unto the angel, "How shall this be, seeing I know not a man?"

And the angel answered and said unto her, "The Holy Ghost shall come upon thee, and the power of the Highest shall overshadow thee. Therefore also that holy thing which shall be born of thee shall be called the Son of God.

"And, behold, thy cousin Elisabeth, she hath also conceived a son in her old age. And this is the sixth month with her, who was called barren. For with God nothing shall be impossible."

And Mary said, "Behold the handmaid of the Lord. Be it unto me according to thy word." And the angel departed from her. Luke 1:26–38

THE ANNUNCIATION

The Magnificat

And Mary said, "My soul doth magnify the Lord. And my spirit hath rejoiced in God my Saviour.

"For he hath regarded the low estate of his handmaiden. For, behold, from henceforth all generations shall call me blessed.

"For he that is mighty hath done to me great things, and holy is his name.

"And his mercy is on them that fear him from generation to generation.

"He hath showed strength with his arm. He hath scattered the proud in the imagination of their hearts.

"He hath put down the mighty from their seats and exalted them of low degree.

"He hath filled the hungry with good things. And the rich he hath sent empty away.

"He hath holpen his servant Israel, in remembrance of his mercy;

"As he spake to our fathers, to Abraham, and to his seed for ever."

Luke 1:46–55

MEDITATION FOR CONCEPTION

I AM Pure[*]

By God's desire from on high,
Accepted now as I draw nigh,
Like falling snow with star-fire glow,
Thy blessed purity does bestow
Its gift of love to me.

I AM pure, pure, pure
By God's own word.
I AM pure, pure, pure,
O fiery sword.
I AM pure, pure, pure,
Truth is adored.

Descend and make me whole,
Blessed Eucharist, fill my soul.
I AM thy law, I AM thy light,
O mold me in thy form so bright!

Beloved I AM! Beloved I AM!
Beloved I AM!

---

[*]As you affirm purity and wholeness, you become a chalice for the descent of the Holy Spirit, which is present at the moment of conception.

I AM Thy Chalice

I AM the true life of the flame,
A focus of God's I AM name,
Descending cycle from the sun,
My radiant source, thou lovely one!

I AM thy chalice ever free—
My purposed aim like thee to be,
A ray of light's expanding love,
A focus for God's comfort dove.

Thy ray now anchored in my form
Does my divinity adorn:
Thy flame, a rising sacred fire,
Each moment takes me ever higher

Until at last made purer still,
Eternal focus of thy will,
I AM thy crystal chalice pure,
An anchor of thy love secure.

A healing fountain to the earth,
I AM real proof of life's rebirth,
Which by the power of thy name
Ascends today thy love to claim.

I AM thy radiance crystal clear,
Forever pouring through me here.
Thy living joy fore'er expanding,
I AM with thee all life commanding!

SEALING OF CONCEPTION:

It Is Finished!*

It is finished!
Thy perfect creation is within me.
Immortally lovely,
It cannot be denied the blessedness of being.
Like unto thyself,
    it abides in the house of reality.
Nevermore to go out into profanity,
It knows only the wonders
    of purity and victory.

---

*You may also choose to memorize this decree and give it every day during pregnancy for your child's protection.

CHAPTER FIVE

The Miracle
of Life
from Conception
Through Birth

The passage from nothing to the complex body of the fully grown individual is one of the constant miracles of life. If we are not struck by the greatness of this miracle, it can only be for one reason, that it occurs so often under our eyes in the experience of everyday life.

—JULIAN S. HUXLEY

Before conceiving my twins, I had a dream that I had three children. In the dream I had twin boys, who appeared as toddlers, and I was holding a baby in my arms. I didn't know what sex the baby was in the dream. But I did end up having three children—twin boys and then a girl.

At the time my husband and I were preparing to conceive my daughter, Marie, I had an interesting thing happen. It was the day after my period and I didn't think I could get pregnant. The next morning my husband asked, "Are you pregnant?"

I said, "Well, no, honey, I can't be pregnant."

He replied, "I don't know. I had a dream that a little girl sent me a Mailgram that said 'Hi, Daddy.'"

That same day my boys were taking a bath and I could see all these colorful lights in the bathroom, so I took a Polaroid picture. And these lights came out in one of the photographs and it looked like a rainbow sphere. It resembled a picture that I had seen depicting the Higher Self. So we always thought that was the presence of the soul of my daughter.

Anyway, I found out I was in fact pregnant. So
I thought it was kind of cute that she let us know that
she was coming.

　　　　　　　✑

Conception Is Phenomenal

The most magnificent drama of life is conducted in the secret world of the mother's womb. The seed of man and woman unite, and from that moment the story of a new life begins. Considering all that has to happen for one sperm cell and one egg cell, or ovum, to meet, it is phenomenal that we even exist.

The female's ovaries contain roughly a million or more immature egg cells at birth. A single ovum ripens each month and is released from the surface of the ovary approximately two weeks before menstruation. The ovum then enters the Fallopian tube. If fertilization doesn't take place within twenty-four hours, the ovum disintegrates and is shed with the uterine lining in menstruation.

Like the egg cells, the sperm cells have a very brief life span of one to two days after leaving the testicles. The short life of both the sperm and egg cells limits the fertile period. Thus the timing of conception is precise, as some parents have intuitively discovered.

　　　　　　　✑

Usually my husband came home late from work.
But on Valentine's Day he was unexpectedly home at
5:00 p.m. So I started to cook dinner for us.

While I was in the kitchen cooking fish on the stove, a strong presence imparted to me through my inner voice, "Turn off the fish, go in and conceive a child!"

I was so surprised because we had been celibate for eight months. But I turned off the fish and went to tell my husband what happened.

He said, "Now?" with a startled laugh.

I said, "Yes."

That evening we conceived a child.

❧

When my first baby was about a year and a half old, I had a very strong sense that another baby was waiting to come. One evening my husband came in after a busy day. He was in bed and I was brushing my teeth. I felt a nudge on my elbow and then someone standing beside me. Impressed on my mind were the words "Tonight is the night."

I went into the bedroom and told my husband what had happened and that we had to do something about it. On that night we did conceive our second daughter.

❧

Sperm cells are tiny—only two-hundredths of an inch in length. They must swim six to seven inches (or 300 to 350 times their length) and through cervical mucus in order for conception to occur. Throughout most of the menstrual cycle, this mucus is thick and sticky, making it very difficult for the sperm to pass through.

However, when ovulation occurs the mucus is clearer and more liquid, and the sperm easily pass through the neck of the uterus. Those sperm which get through seek the ovum with determination. The first sperm to reach the ovum is drawn in. The ovum's cell membrane then rapidly changes and all other sperm are kept out.

The sperm nucleus and egg nucleus unite and the ovum is fertilized. The genetic material from both parents is combined. Within a day, two new nuclei are formed and the fertilized cell divides. The baby's life begins.

༄

The most remarkable experiences I have had with my pregnancies were when I felt the actual conception of my children take place. This was not during intercourse but about sixteen hours afterward in both cases.

I was in the kitchen cooking one morning when suddenly I felt the most wonderful sense of joy. I was so inexplicably buoyant and happy that I called my husband to tell him I didn't know what had happened but I felt so happy.

We had been trying to conceive for over a year and I had a history of reproductive problems that made pregnancy unlikely. I didn't connect this experience with conception until a couple of weeks later when I found out that I was indeed pregnant. I'll never forget that day and the feeling of joy!

With my second pregnancy I was sitting at lunch with my first daughter, who was then a toddler. It was the second month that we had been trying to conceive again. I had ovulated over the weekend and was waiting for signs of pregnancy.

This time I felt a shower of light so tangible that it startled me. I knew instantly that I had just conceived again, and I turned to look at the clock to see exactly what the time was. Within a couple of weeks the pregnancy was confirmed.

❧

It was a radiant, sunny day. I was going to a baby shower for a good friend and had bought some nice gifts for her. I also had one very special item that I had used for some of my children that I was wrapping.

I suddenly stopped and looked at it. The sun was shining through the window right on it. I felt a ray of spiritual light come down as well. At that moment, I immediately knew that I had just conceived another child—and I had.

❧

God Endows Every Living Cell with Freedom

Guided by the inner blueprint of creation, the fertilized cell rapidly divides and moves down the Fallopian tube into the uterus. By the time the cells reach the uterus, they have become a tiny human embryo.* The embryo then attaches to the soft uterine lining for shelter and nourishment.

From that point on, the embryo significantly influences the pregnancy. He helps develop his own life-support system (the placenta), which produces many hormones that sustain the pregnancy. And he eventually regulates the volume of his amniotic fluid by drinking it. The fetus also determines his position in the womb, the time labor begins and the moment of birth. These are no small accomplishments.

To me, the fetus is nothing less than a god—God in manifestation in all of his glory. And how gloriously the fetus reflects the individualization of God in man. How reverently God endows us from conception with a sense of mission, with individual responsibility, with the need to be self-determined beings, with the need to fight for life and to perform all the vital functions in the womb.

Why did God, as Creator, ensure that the fetus would have all of these functions? God could just as well

---

*The developing baby in the womb is referred to as an *embryo* until the end of the eighth week after conception. From nine weeks after conception to birth, the unborn baby is called a *fetus*.

have created various systems in the mother's body to perform all of these functions for the baby.

I believe it is because God endows us with freedom from the moment of conception. There is even freedom inherent in the fact that of the millions of sperm released, only the one most able and most determined will fertilize that egg. Every part of life—down to a single cell—is endowed with freedom. And when we realize this and also think of the precision involved in the formation of the baby's body, we are in awe of life.

Maria Montessori, who was trained as a medical doctor before she did her pioneering work in education, had a profound understanding and respect for the child aborning in the womb and for his creator. She said:

> Parents, especially the mother, are vividly conscious that they have played an insignificant part in the process of conception and birth, compared with that accomplished by nature. . . . It is not the mother who brings about the growth of the child in her womb; this is accomplished by the power of the same Being who created it in her. Nor is it the mother who accomplishes the birth of the baby; this marvelous act is performed by nature and only seconded by the mother.
>
> It is just because God has fixed the manner of conception, development and birth in this way that the parents feel such a deep natural

respect in the presence of this child who has come to them in this mysterious fashion. This respect is increased when they realize another truth—that the principal part of man, his soul, does not come from man at all, but is created directly by God.[1]

The Baby's Rapid Development and Repertoire of Movements*

About three weeks after conception, the baby's heart begins to beat. As early as week four, major divisions of the brain are forming. By the seventh week, the face has eyes, ears, nose, tongue and lips. During the eighth week, the arms and legs show their first tiny movements, and all the internal organs have started to develop.

During the third month, the baby begins to be very active. His muscles mature, giving him a full repertoire of movements. He can stretch his limbs, kick his feet, curl his toes, turn his head, squint his eyes, move his fingers, suck his thumb, and open and close his mouth.

When the fetus is about four months old, the mother may begin to feel the baby's movements. These movements are now more spontaneous, coordinated and complex.

During the fifth month, the baby will gain a lot of weight and grow to half its birth length. From twenty

*For a complete outline of fetal development, see appendix A.

weeks until birth, all the organs will continue to grow and refine.

By the end of the sixth month, weighing about two pounds, the unborn baby is essentially the same as the baby at birth. The baby even sleeps and wakes in cycles similar to a newborn and has his favorite sleeping position. Often the mother's sleep habits are transferred to the baby. He's awake when she's awake; he's asleep when she's asleep. However, that is not always the case.

⤙

When I was pregnant, my baby would start to play a lot and become more active at my bedtime. So I often had to tell her to settle down so I could go to sleep. When that didn't work, my husband would talk to her. She always obeyed him!

⤙

During the early stages of pregnancy, the fetus is free to move as he pleases. He is in a situation much akin to that of an astronaut in space. He can turn complete flips and perform other complex movements that develop muscles and nerve pathways to the brain. Even in late pregnancy, the fetus will change position in order to be more comfortable. As the baby shifts, stretches and changes position, the mother may find a small lump on her abdomen—often an elbow or a foot!

⤙

Toward the end of my pregnancy, my baby had a foot on one of my organs, causing me a great deal of pain. This went on for several days.

My husband finally talked to her in a voice of gentle authority. He said: "You need to move. You're causing Mama pain and you have to move into another position."

She responded right away. The relief was tremendous. This was one example of her gracious, kind soul.

‿

The Soul Comes Down the Spiritual Birth Canal

The overriding presence of the soul for whom the body is being prepared within the womb is magnificent to behold. From the moment of conception, the child's soul is an active participant in forming the body she is to inhabit to fulfill her mission in life.

Throughout the entire nine months of gestation, the soul may go back and forth from her body in the womb to higher planes of existence in the heaven-world. Each time the soul enters her body she anchors more of her soul substance in that body. As gestation progresses, the spirit, or the essence, of the soul becomes a part of the blood and the cells—a part of the brain, the heart and all of the organs.

At the moment of birth (the timing of which is integral to the soul's mission), the soul comes down the spiritual birth canal, which is like a large funnel. You can think of this spiritual birth canal as a descending spiral from God. It comes right down to the place where the baby's physical body is prepared.

～

I was attending the birth of my friend Alice's child. Just before the midwife announced the baby was crowning, I had a vision of what was happening spiritually in that birth.

Alice was lying on a marble altar and around the altar were twelve spiritual beings. They looked like angels or saints. A beam of light came down from above and passed through Alice. Then I saw the baby come floating down through the beam toward her womb.

I heard an inner voice say, "This is happening as the baby is coming down the birth canal." After this, the baby crowned and was born without difficulty.

～

My late husband Mark Prophet told me that he remembered his birth, which was on Christmas Eve 1918. He remembered coming over the little town where his mother was in labor and watching his father cross the bridge to go home to be with her. And he remembered coming down in a vortex of light and actually entering his physical body.

The soul is fully integrated with the body at the moment of birth, and a curtain of forgetfulness is drawn over the memory body of the soul at that time. The soul then no longer has full memory of her preexistence in the heaven-world or in past lives.

Childbirth Is a Rite of Passage

When I was almost due, I was asleep and heard a voice say, "Mother, it's time to go." I hadn't broken my waters yet, but I woke my husband up, told him what had happened and prepared to leave.

We had barely reached the place where I was going to deliver when I felt the baby's head crowning. The baby popped out soon after that.

I believe my child woke me up so I wouldn't give birth to him in the car.

⌐

The childbirth experience is an initiation for both the baby and the parents. It is a rite of passage for the soul of the child entering physical existence. And it is a rite of passage for the parents. The woman takes on the role of mother and the man takes on the role of father.

Childbirth is also an initiation which requires the mother to yield—to surrender to a force of nature outside her conscious control. The father's involvement or role in the childbirth process differs for every couple. The very nature of this initiation requires both parents to reach deep within themselves to discover hidden resources of strength and purpose. In this process they are raised to new heights of maturity.

While childbirth has spiritual meanings, it is nonetheless a physical experience. More than that, it is an experience that is unique to every woman. A woman brings to the birth all that she is—spiritually, mentally, emotionally and physically.

So when the mother goes into labor, she can meditate in her heart and trust in the birth wisdom of her body. As she maintains a posture of listening grace through relaxation techniques and meditation on her breath, the goal is to allow herself to open to the strength that is working through her. She will naturally respond to the rhythm of her body in a way that is unique to her.

Regardless of whether the baby is delivered naturally or with medical intervention, something wondrous takes place through the travail of giving birth. The woman experiences the dominion of self, of ultimately fulfilling the function of life and, yes, a certain amount of discomfort, inconvenience and pain. But when we understand it, the suffering of pain can be positive. It impels us to a higher awareness of God and enables us to balance karma in the process.

When a child is being born, the woman bears the supreme effort and involvement of cosmic forces passing through her in the creative tension and concentration of energy in her contractions. She also experiences the glorious release when that tension is ended and in her arms is a living child!

⌒

During the weeks prior to giving birth, I would look over and over at very explicit photos of a baby being born. I worked on processing my feelings surrounding the birth—for example, my disbelief in my body's ability to open up and to allow the baby through—and surrendering my baby to that birth process. One day I finished this work and the last vestige of fear or holding back left me, and I really believed my body could handle the birth.

A couple of days before the baby came I saw the movie Black Beauty, *which showed the birth of a foal. I thought of how animals give birth and appear to surrender to the process. They do not seem to fear it. It helped me trust in what was to happen.*

During labor the strength and the surges my body was responding to were magnificent. I stayed in the role of trusting and observing and did not hinder the process.

My mind went completely still and, as with all my births, my Higher Self every now and again impressed some helpful tip on my mind. Any time a trace of fear entered my mind, I did notice "pain" in my cervix instead of a tremendous opening. The image of a tree came into my mind—its strength and flexibility—bending with the wind!

I was amazed at my body's ability to open. I kept the visualization in my mind of the cervix opening, remembering to let myself open. I was by myself at the time and was able to keep my concentration.

When the baby arrived, I felt that I had experienced little or no pain, just the extraordinary workings of my body governed by something greater than myself. I felt great joy to have been part of this process.

〰

I had a very difficult birth with my son, Alexander. The first part of labor was without problems. When I was almost completely dilated, I saw three cherubs on my bed and a circle of about seven magnificent white angels around the bed. One was standing near the door.

I asked this angel, "Who are you?"

The angel responded: "A sentry. I am guarding the coming of Alexander."

I felt as if I was lying on an "altar of birth" with the cherubs sitting next to me. The other angels stood around me. The baby was descending through a crystal cord that was above me. Then I saw three saints at the foot of my bed having a conversation. They communicated to me that the easy part of the birth was over and that now it was going to get difficult.

The next four hours were in fact very difficult for both me and my son. The difficulty of this experience was clearly a karmic package that we had chosen to balance together. But during that time, I unexpectedly felt at peace and totally calm.

⤺

Protection for Your Baby

The importance of giving prayers and meditations for the protection of your baby from conception through birth cannot be overemphasized. Fathers are especially good at keeping this vigil of protection.

You can establish a shield of protection daily for yourself, your spouse and your baby by giving the Meditation for Protection at the end of this chapter. And you can ask God to send his angels to protect you. Thousands of people have experienced miracles that they believe were made possible by their relationship with angels.

One angel you should know by name is Archangel Michael. He is the greatest and most revered angel in Jewish, Christian and Islamic tradition. He and the legions of angels he commands protect us from physical and spiritual dangers—everything from accidents, burglaries and rape to the ravages of terrorism and war. Archangel Michael has personally saved my life a dozen times that I know of and probably thousands of times that I am not aware of. I am sure the same is true for you.

On the following pages, you will find decrees for protection that you can give to call Archangel Michael into action in your life.[2] They are meant to be said aloud—even shouted in situations of serious danger. Your call can be as simple as: "Archangel Michael, help me! Help me! Help me!"

〜

I remember an almost painless birth with my son. The only thing that was uncomfortable was a burning sensation at the very end.

I prayed out loud to Archangel Michael during delivery. All the staff at the hospital were wondering what I was doing and saying. Some were amazed at how effortless and painless the birth was. One nurse said, "Whatever she's doing, it's working!"

The entire process was incredible and swift, which I attribute to my prayers to Archangel Michael and my son's strong desire to be here. I was also in excellent physical condition. (I taught aerobics just before pregnancy.) Although my son was three weeks early, he was a healthy, easygoing, eight-pound baby.

〜

Meditation for Protection

VISUALIZATION:

As you give the following decree, see God's light descending into your heart, body, mind and soul. See this light intensify in your heart as a blazing sun, a sphere of white light. Then see it expanding from your heart to create a large sphere of light, a shield of protection, that extends around your body in all directions.

DECREE:

O mighty presence of God, I AM,
    in and behind the sun:
I welcome thy light,
    which floods all the earth,
    into my life, into my mind,
    into my spirit, into my soul.
Radiate and blaze forth thy light!
Break the bonds of darkness and superstition!
Charge me with the great clearness
    of thy white fire radiance!
I AM thy child, and each day I shall become
    more of thy manifestation!

MEDITATION FOR PROTECTION

See Archangel Michael as a beautiful, powerful and majestic angel arrayed in shining armor with a brilliant sapphire blue cape and aura. See him standing before you, behind you, to your right, to your left, above, beneath and in the center of your body. He is always accompanied by limitless numbers of angels who will protect and escort you wherever you go. See him wielding a sword of blue flame to protect you and your unborn baby from all physical and spiritual dangers.

DECREE:

Lord Michael before,
Lord Michael behind,
Lord Michael to the right,
Lord Michael to the left,
Lord Michael above,
Lord Michael below,
Lord Michael, Lord Michael wherever I go!

I AM his love protecting here!
I AM his love protecting here!
I AM his love protecting here!

ARCHANGEL MICHAEL

DECREE:

Guard, guard, guard us!
 By the lightning of thy love!
Guard, guard, guard us!
 By thy great Self above!
Guard, guard, guard us!
 By thy secret power of light!
Guard, guard, guard us!
 By thy great and glorious might!
And seal us safe forever
 In thy diamond heart of light!

CHAPTER SIX

You Can Help
Change Your
Child's Karma

When we recognize in the appeal of nature, the appeal of God Himself summoning us to assist the child, then we shall always be ready to comply with the child's needs. Then we shall see how, in this way, we are placing ourselves at the service of God's plans and collaborating with the work of God in the child.

—MARIA MONTESSORI

As parents-to-be, you have a unique opportunity to assist the soul of your child before birth, and even before conception. You can commune with the Higher Self of your unborn baby as you give violet-flame decrees to transmute, or erase, portions of his negative karma.

As discussed in chapter 1, the soul carries records of karma with her from lifetime to lifetime. These include both positive and negative patterns of thinking and feeling. Negative patterns can sometimes deter a soul from making right choices just because she is in the habit of thinking or feeling a certain way. These habits can ultimately deter her from choosing to fulfill her mission in life. Thus, a parent's spiritual work to help transmute the negative karmic patterns of the unborn child is a profound service of love.

Erase Painful Memories of Your Child's Past Lives

The soul of your child will receive the most benefit if you give violet-flame decrees for her before birth. However, your decrees can be effective at any time during her development—even months before conception or years after birth. It is never too early or too late to invoke the violet flame for your child, because the violet flame can erase karmic records and memories retroactively throughout all past lives.

After you have been giving the violet flame for some time, you may find yourself recalling glimpses of your child's past lives. You may have a dream or an intuition about your child as he was in ages long past. Or you may just have an impression that he was in a particular time or place.

Shortly after my second son was born, my wife and I found out that he was not too fond of baths. We knew that many babies cried during baths, but our son's reaction to baths was extreme. Even though we took great care to hold him secure in his little bathtub, he would fight, scream, kick and pinch. He was clearly terrified by the water. So we had to resort to sponge bathing him for several months.

Since we knew our baby had not had any traumatic experiences with water in his short life to cause such a reaction, we realized that he must have been experiencing some type of memory from a past life. We also realized then that perhaps it was no coincidence that both his first and middle names referred to the sea. And then my wife had a dream about his drowning.

Even as a newborn baby, this child had a strong and domineering personality. Thus, because of all these factors, we could easily, almost humorously, imagine him in a previous life as the captain of a ship. And sadly, perhaps the ship sank and he drowned. But whatever his past trauma was with water, we are grateful to have had the violet flame to help him through these memories.

I think our awareness of this experience and belief in reincarnation also enabled us to be more sensitive to his fear of water as he got older. He was very cautious and slow to learn how to swim, but we never pressured him. Now at ten years old he seems happy and confident in a swimming pool. The bad memories appear to be gone.

🍃

Memories of past lives are still dimly present for most children until age three or so. They don't necessarily understand what they are seeing or remembering. They often do not articulate it, even to their parents. They think their visions and memories of past lives are what life is all about—that we all remember who we are and where we came from. Sometimes the past-life memories children have are interesting and joyful, and other times they are painful.

🍃

This is not an easy story to tell. My third child almost starved to death when he was a baby and a toddler. He was hungry all the time but kept spitting up and was unable to assimilate his food. He received

*chiropractic adjustments and consistent care from his
father, and eventually he began to thrive.*

*He is now four years old, but he's still almost
always hungry. He talks about food constantly.
Recently I asked him why he worries about having
enough food.*

*"I starved to death," he told me. And then he
started to cry. "I don't want my head to get too big,"
he said. "Once before my head got too big and my
body too small, and my head fell off. I was a baby and
didn't have enough food and I didn't have a mother."
He hung his head down on his chest to show me.*

*Normally he is a very happy boy and has always
been drawn to Tibetan music, books and pictures. As
a baby he would bring out the Tibetan books and
show them to a friend of ours. He had no idea our
friend was connected to Tibet. I am sure our son was
recently embodied in Tibet and probably did starve to
death there.*

↜

If the memories are painful—and they often are
because the soul is crying out for resolution—you or
your child may feel sadness or regret. But you will also
feel liberated as you give violet-flame decrees because
you know you are clearing the records of karma. And if
your child is old enough to decree, it is preferable to give
these violet-flame decrees together.

So if you become aware of these memories, don't try to suppress them. Instead, focus your attention on the light in your heart. Imagine the experience being saturated with the violet flame until the image disappears from before your inner eye. Then let go of the memory and see a bright white sun replace the image in your mind's eye.

Past-life records and memories are like files on the computer of the subconscious mind. You need to erase them in order to make room for positive programming. As you do so through the violet flame, you are freeing your child's soul to move on to higher levels of existence.

Violet Flame for Healing

The violet flame can also transmute the cause of unhealthy conditions or weakness in the baby's body, which may be the result of negative karma. And it can miraculously assist in the healing of problems in the developing organs of the baby during gestation.

⤳

During pregnancy I had an ultrasound which revealed that my baby had an extra large kidney, indicative of a weak or deformed heart. When I found this out, I increased my violet-flame decrees for her healing. For five months we followed her progress on the ultrasounds, and there was no change in the condition of her kidney.

*My due date came and went. So one day I went
alone into our sanctuary room and began doing
rosaries to the Virgin Mary. I ended the prayer ses-
sion with violet-flame decrees.*

*Early the next morning I went into labor, but
before going to the hospital I gave the Hail Mary.
When I got to the hospital my labor was fast, just two
hours. When the pediatrician checked my baby, she no
longer had an enlarged kidney and her heart was fine.*

*What a miracle! I believe that the Virgin Mary
and the violet flame healed my beautiful daughter.*

⤳

*During my third pregnancy, I had a lot of emo-
tional turmoil in my family. We were helping to take
care of two foster children who had psychological problems. I felt that I didn't have enough time to commune
with my baby as I had done in previous pregnancies.
And I had a lot more stress. It seemed like the pregnancy went by without my giving it a lot of time.*

*But in the midst of all this, I did give a lot of
violet-flame decrees. My daughter was born with a
strong physical constitution and personality.*

*To this day, she remains very healthy and has an
inquisitive and honest personality, with a strong sense
of justice. This pregnancy was a lesson in trust for
me, and I believe the violet flame really helped!*

⤳

Invoking the violet flame is the most important spiritual exercise you can do for your child before birth—and after birth as well. And when you give violet-flame decrees for your child, make your prayers specific. At the end of this chapter, you will find examples of specific prayers you can give for your child prior to conception and during pregnancy. These prayers can help promote the highest development of your baby's four "bodies."

Purify the Etheric Body of Your Child

Did you know that your baby will actually have four bodies, not just one? The four bodies are the etheric body (the memory), the mental body (the mind), the emotional body (the feelings and desires) and the physical body.

One very important prayer to give, ideally three months or more before conception, is that the soul assigned to your family receive the benefit of your violet-flame decrees for the purification of her etheric body. The importance of this specific prayer cannot be overemphasized. Everything that your child will be comes out of his etheric body.

The etheric body, also called the envelope of the soul, travels with the soul from lifetime to lifetime. The other three bodies disintegrate at the end of each life and are reformed during gestation and the formative years.

The etheric body has two parts. The higher etheric body contains the blueprint of our identity in God. The lower etheric body contains the records of our past lives. Out of the lower etheric body will come the manifestation of karmic patterns in the mental, emotional and physical bodies. Thus our mind, emotions and physical bodies often do not reflect the original blueprint of our soul's identity in God—they reflect our karma.

Since most of us have had many past lives, our etheric bodies are often very dense with records of karma we have made. So the mental body, for example, will generally be fashioned after the mental body of the previous life and the one before that and the one before that. Invoking the violet flame for your child before conception can help erase karmic patterns in his etheric body that would limit his capacity to express his innate potential in life.

It is sad but true that we are all limited by our four bodies and by the karma manifest in them. Until we mature, give service to life, use the violet flame and purify ourselves, we are greatly hampered by our bodies and the habit patterns of past lives. Regular use of the violet flame can clear away certain misuses of the memory, the mind, the emotions and the physical body. This you can do on behalf of your child.

Imagine the perfection of your child's soul in its purest state when her first mental body and her first emotional body and her first physical body were created according to the original blueprint. This is a very powerful visualization.

❧

When I was four weeks pregnant, I became quite ill. There was virtually nothing I could eat without getting a severe stomachache and sometimes diarrhea or a headache as well. I had already missed ten days of work, I was losing weight and I was sleeping about twenty hours a day. At that point, I honestly feared that either I or the baby was not going to survive.

I woke up just before dawn on Christmas Day with a sudden and clear conviction. I felt that I had been given a divine revelation: I needed to do one thousand hours of violet flame! In return I asked for my own healing and for the transmutation of anything that would interfere with the perfect blueprint of the four bodies of my child. I also offered to God that he could use my decrees for the salvation of souls or for problems in the world if these were the greater need.

I determined to complete the vigil over the course of the next three years. At that rate, I would average just under an hour of violet flame each day. However, I set my heart and mind on fulfilling my promise as quickly as possible. I aimed for three hours a day during my pregnancy. In order to accomplish this, I had to forgo all movies, socializing, listening to

music and even reading books, with very few excep-
tions. When I was too sick to go to work, I would
simply decree all day as I lay in bed.

The pregnancy continued to be quite difficult for
a few months, but eventually I was back at work. In
August my daughter was born. From the very beginning, she was a child of remarkable peace, beauty and
joy. She has a very quick mind and a sweet disposi-
tion. She also has had exceptionally good health. My
husband and I are grateful beyond words for the great
happiness and abundant laughter she has brought to
our home.

The result of this violet-flame vigil has also been
a wonderful transformation for me personally. Blocks
in my psychology and in my relationship with my parents and sisters and brother dissolved miraculously.
My relationship with my husband became far more
loving and harmonious.

Our financial situation also improved dramatically. We were given a number of generous gifts by
our families and friends. And we were somehow able
to pay all of the expenses related to the pregnancy and
birth.

I completed the one thousand hours of violet-
flame decrees for my first child before my second child
was born. Even though my physical condition had not
changed yet, everything else had improved so much

I decided to give the same amount of violet-flame decrees for my next child.

So I became pregnant again and partway through the second violet-flame vigil, about six months after our son's birth, I found out what my physical problem was. I had a hereditary disease that causes a severe reaction to certain foods. This diagnosis was miraculous. It meant going from being in constant pain to something that is now controllable through my diet. I have been so blessed by this entire experience that I am determined, by God's grace, to give a thousand hours of violet flame for each and every child God sends to our family!

ᔐ

Give Specific Prayers for Each Trimester

You can give specific prayers with your violet-flame decrees asking God to assist the soul of your child to transmute her weaknesses and negative karma, trimester by trimester (see prayers at the end of this chapter). Through these devotions, you can help prevent your child's negative karma from affecting him.

The diagram on the following page shows the development of your child's four bodies in relation to the trimesters of gestation. It demonstrates at what stage, beginning with conception, the child will draw into his mind, emotions and physical body his strengths and weaknesses from past lives. Strengths and weaknesses in the mental, emotional and physical bodies of the parents may also be passed on to the child at these stages.

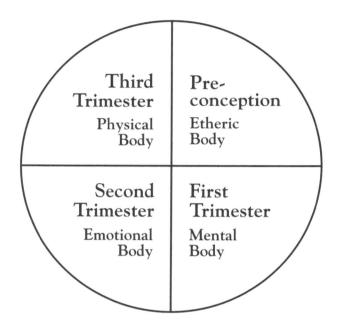

The first trimester (conception to three months) represents the major development of the child's mind and will. The parents' (and especially the mother's) mental abilities, tendencies and willpower greatly affect this period of development in the child.

The second trimester (three to six months) represents the major development of the emotional body. Stable and unstable tendencies can begin at this time and are highly influenced by the mother's emotions and her environment, including the kind of music she hears, the people she interacts with, and the movies and other things she observes.

The third trimester (six months to birth) represents the major growth and development of the physical body. Throughout pregnancy, but especially in the third trimester, the mother's nutrition is all-important. The baby's brain and body are developing rapidly during this time.

⌒

With my third child, I learned to go to an inner place in my heart and commune with the baby's soul. Often I would ask the baby many questions about what he or she needed. During these times, I saw my baby as a simple monk dressed in brown robes, sitting under a tree meditating. We would often sit and meditate together.

What was very interesting is how he communicated what kinds of prayers he wanted me to do during pregnancy. There was a definite pattern that correlated with the trimesters! During my first trimester, he wanted a lot of decrees done for protection. In the second trimester, he asked for devotions for wisdom and illumination. And during the third trimester, the emphasis was on love.

⌒

The following are examples of prayers you can give with violet-flame decrees for yourself and your child before conception and during pregnancy. Be creative with your prayers and make them specific to your own situation.

PRAYERS:

In the name of God I AM THAT I AM and according to God's will, I call for:

- the purification of my child's etheric body so that his (her) mental, emotional and physical bodies will be formed according to the original blueprint of the soul

- the transmutation of my child's negative karma, any negative karma I may have with this child and the negative karma this child has with any member of my family

- the transmutation of all that would oppose the fulfillment of the mission and highest potential of my child.

PRAYERS FOR THE FIRST TRIMESTER:

In the name of God I AM THAT I AM
and according to God's will, I call for:

- the protection of the perfect formation of all organ structures being developed in my baby at this time

- the transmutation of any negative karma that would impede the perfect development of my baby's mind and will

- the transference of God's mind and God's will to my baby

- the transmutation of any hereditary weaknesses in my mental abilities or willpower that would adversely affect my baby.

In the name of God I AM THAT I AM
and according to God's will, I call for:

* the protection of the development of my baby's brain and skeletal system and for the continuing rapid growth of all the organs and perfect body features

* the transmutation of any negative karma that would impede the perfect development and peace of my baby's emotional body

* the transference of God's peace and harmony to my baby's feelings

* the transmutation of any hereditary weaknesses in my feelings and desires that would adversely affect my baby.

In the name of God I AM THAT I AM
and according to God's will, I call for:

- the protection of the development of my baby, especially the refinement of the eyes, ears, nose, heart, lungs, brain, skin and digestive tract

- the transmutation of any negative karma that would impede the perfect development and beauty of my baby's physical body

- the transference of God's perfection and healing to my baby's physical body

- the transmutation of any hereditary weaknesses or undesirable physical conditions that would affect my baby, including _____

- the protection of the birth of my child (including the midwife, doctors, nurses and hospital technicians).

VISUALIZATION:

Visualize yourself and your child surrounded by violet flames, rising and pulsating around you as you decree. See these flames pass through your body, restoring wholeness. See them saturating your mind and your emotions, relieving all your burdens. Then see these flames saturating the soul of your child and her etheric, mental, emotional and physical bodies.

PREAMBLE:

In the name of God I AM THAT I AM
and according to God's will, I decree:

DECREE:

I AM the violet flame
In action in me now
I AM the violet flame
To light alone I bow
I AM the violet flame
In mighty cosmic power
I AM the light of God
Shining every hour
I AM the violet flame
Blazing like a sun
I AM God's sacred power
Freeing every one

DECREE:

Radiant spiral violet flame,
  Descend, now blaze through me!
Radiant spiral violet flame,
  Set free, set free, set free!

Radiant violet flame, O come,
  Expand and blaze thy light through me!
Radiant violet flame, O come,
  Reveal God's power for all to see!
Radiant violet flame, O come,
  Awake the earth and set it free!

Radiance of the violet flame,
  Expand and blaze through me!
Radiance of the violet flame,
  Expand for all to see!
Radiance of the violet flame,
  Establish mercy's outpost here!
Radiance of the violet flame,
  Come, transmute now all fear!

DECREE:

Violet flame from the heart of God, (3x*)
 Expand thy mercy through me today! (3x)
Violet flame from the heart of God, (3x)
 Transmute all wrong by forgiveness ray! (3x)
Violet flame from the heart of God, (3x)
 Blaze into action through all to stay! (3x)
Violet flame from the heart of God, (3x)
 O mercy's flame, fore'er hold sway! (3x)
Violet flame from the heart of God, (3x)
 Sweep all the earth by Christ-command! (3x)
Violet flame from the heart of God, (3x)
 Thy freeing power I now demand! (3x)

Take dominion now,
To thy light I bow;
I AM thy radiant light,
Violet flame so bright.
Grateful for thy ray
Sent to me today,
Fill me through and through
Until there's only you!

---

*"3x" means to give each line three times.

DECREE:

> Breath of God inside each cell
> I AM the violet flame
> Pulsing out the cosmic time
> I AM the violet flame
> Energizing mind and heart
> I AM the violet flame
> Sustaining God's creation now
> I AM the violet flame
>
> With all love
> With all love
> With all love
>
> Shimmering in a crystal cave
> I AM the violet flame
> Searching out all hidden pain
> I AM the violet flame
> Consuming cause and core of fear
> I AM the violet flame
> Revealing now the inner name
> I AM the violet flame

(decree continues)

decree (continued)

> With all peace
> With all peace
> With all peace
>
> Flashing like a lightning bolt
> I AM the violet flame
> Stretching through the galaxies
> I AM the violet flame
> Connecting soul and spirit now
> I AM the violet flame
> Raising you to cosmic heights
> I AM the violet flame
>
> With all power
> With all power
> With all power

CHAPTER SEVEN

Spiritual Heredity

The Will, feeling, desire and active effort, on the part of the pregnant woman, may completely reverse *heredity and natural tendencies, not to mention future possibilities.*

—R. SWINBURNE CLYMER

J ust as the child's karmic patterns from past lives affect the formation of his four bodies, so do they influence the traits that he inherits. Hereditary traits represent qualities and potentials. And how they manifest is governed by the interaction of consciousness, environment, karma and the innate pattern.

Hereditary traits are carried by both parents, although they don't necessarily show up in the parents. But we do not merely inherit these traits from our parents; exceptional talents and intelligence are the sign of many lifetimes of concentrating on a particular ability and mastering it. This is why we often see children with qualities that apparently did not come from their parents. The children bring their own heredity with them and remold themselves after their own divine image.

You Can Change Your Child's Heredity

Hereditary traits are conveyed by the genes. The genes are contained in threadlike structures called chromosomes, which are found in the nuclei of the cells. In man there are twenty-three pairs of chromosomes, or forty-six altogether.

A normal undivided chromosome contains a single DNA (deoxyribonucleic acid) molecule known as the double helix. This molecule has a simple structure—two intertwined coils in which the genes are arranged in linear order. The coils are connected by rungs at regular intervals, creating what looks like a spiral staircase.

We know that DNA can be damaged by environmental agents such as chemicals, radiation and viruses.[1] If your DNA can be damaged by these agents, can't it also be healed and transformed by the tremendous force of light from your Higher Self?

Let us consider for a moment the factors that, generation after generation, direct the quality of life within the genes. The genes produce the differentiation of our physical nature and even retain some remnant of our character traits from previous lives.

Let us look at the substance that God has placed in the sperm and in the egg, each one contributing twenty-three chromosomes to the embryo. The forty-six chromosomes contain the information that determines our physical attributes—everything from the color of our eyes and the texture of our hair to our stature, our body build, mentality, dexterity, thought processes and attitudes.

If both you and your spouse work on the purification of your genes and chromosomes several months before conception, you may be able to transfer more desirable qualities to your child. By giving violet-flame decrees, you can transmute undesirable hereditary traits.

This violet-flame transmutation of one's genes and chromosomes is the only lawful genetic engineering there is. This is because the violet flame is the action of the Holy Spirit, and it only works in accordance with the laws of God. Violet-flame transmutation of the DNA molecule is where true science and the mysteries of God converge. It is the spiritual science of genetic engineering.

Impress Virtues upon the DNA Molecule

A meditation you can do to purify your genes is to take a diagram of the DNA molecule and write on it the virtues and traits that you desire to see expressed in yourself and in your child. (See the diagram at the end of this chapter.) Having a visual image of this molecule gives you the power to influence it. As you meditate on the DNA molecule and give your violet-flame decrees, visualize the violet flame purifying and infusing that molecule with those virtuous qualities.

The three most important virtues that you want to impress upon the DNA molecule are love, wisdom and power. These are the three primary virtues of the flame of God in your heart.

The color vibration that is associated with love is pink. Wisdom is yellow and power is blue. After you give your DNA molecule meditation with violet-flame decrees, you can visualize the color vibrations of these three virtues infusing that molecule.

❧

During both of my pregnancies, I made a meditation book for the baby with my hopes for that child. On a picture of the DNA chain, I wrote the qualities that I wanted for them. I put color overlays on top of the pictures. For example, I used a violet overlay for the DNA chain and fetal development pictures. And I used a yellow overlay for pictures of the brain.

❧

There is no limit to what your mind can impress upon the DNA molecule, the genes and the chromosomes if you begin to think and meditate on God and imagine what the ideal man or woman is intended to be. Pregnancy is a wonderful time to read stories about people of great courage and valor and to center your thoughts on the development of strong character traits within your child.

And it is a time to look at yourself and see what positive qualities you are manifesting. These are the qualities that you will undoubtedly have the greatest ability to convey to your child. Then look at your weaknesses. Look at the traits you wouldn't want anyone else to have, the ones you are trying to overcome. Invoke the violet flame to pass through the DNA molecule for the transmutation of those traits and pray that they will not be transferred to your child.

You can also pray for God's love to be focused in your heart to magnetize virtue from your Higher Self. Ask God to remove all error from your subconscious and unconscious minds so that it will not be passed on to your children and your children's children.

Genes Can Reflect the Genius of the Mind

By our thoughts, we are constantly re-creating the molecules of the mind, and this re-creation is reflected in our genes! The genes themselves carry the momentum of consciousness.

This is why if conception takes place in love and in adoration of God, those qualities will be transmitted to the child. And therefore we realize that the patterns of the soul and the mental, emotional and physical bodies are not set in stone. The genes are the most sensitive vessels of your entire world, and they affect your thinking even as your thinking affects them.

So the stamp of your identity goes forth moment by moment. And you can actually increase your capacity to bear children who have exceptional talents and an extraordinary mission by your self-mastery on a single point of consciousness. This self-mastery is reinforced by your determination not to give up until the desired end is reached.

This tells you something about the power of thought
and feeling and the power of light in your chakras. It
tells you about the power of God in you. It tells you
about the genius of the mind that has its correlation in
the genes of the body. And it tells you about the negative power of idle thoughts and subtle feelings that can
tear from you the momentum of your mission in life. It
all depends upon the impressions of your mind upon the
genes at any given moment.

Passing On Spiritual Qualities

What is not generally known about heredity is that just
as a miniature replica of physical man is contained in
his genes, so the spiritual blueprint, the formula of his
relationship to God, is stamped on the etheric counter-
part of his genetic code. As lifetime follows lifetime, the
spiritual gifts and graces that a soul earns, though they
may be dormant for a season, cannot be lost unless the
soul relinquishes them by free will.

We read in the writings of the apostle Paul about the
passing on of spiritual hereditary qualities, whether
through the genes and chromosomes or by some other
means: "The unfeigned faith that is in thee dwelt first in
thy grandmother Lois and thy mother Eunice."[2]

Children born to parents who are spiritually
inclined may be strengthened in externalizing their
heavenly patterns. This is done through the passing on

of spiritual traits and the transfer of the light of the chakras from one or both parents to the child. This is another reason that the exercise for the purification of the chakras at the end of chapter 3 is so important.

The pure light that the parents carry in their chakras and surrounding their bodies nurtures the soul of the child from conception throughout life. It provides the optimum conditions and environment for the child to realize his fullest potential. Nevertheless, in order to retain the highest qualities and virtues, the child must internalize these virtues on his own.

As parents, you can be the instruments of the Holy Spirit in all that you do. Your children, as well as your projects and endeavors, can receive through you a measure of heavenly light. So don't sell short your potential as a progenitor of God. Even as you daily re-create yourself after the perfect design, you can pass on these virtues to your children!

ᝐ

With my second child, I meditated upon a beautiful picture of the Golden Buddha, which I had found on a recent trip to Malaysia. Intuitively I felt that this was the essence of the child. I also felt compelled to look at and study all sorts of art books, especially those from Russian artists. When our daughter was born, she had a very round face and her eyes looked slightly oriental. She had such a presence of peacefulness about her—just like the Golden Buddha!

ᝐ

The Law of Karma Is Precise

But remember, you can't do it all for your child. Your child can receive a *measure* of God's light through you as you desire to pass on spiritual qualities and to help transmute his negative karma. But it's simply not possible to transmute *all* of it. Nor is it always possible to erase or correct undesirable hereditary traits. There are certain conditions of karma that must be worked out by the soul in physical ways. And these conditions are part of that soul's mission in life.

Have you ever wondered why one baby is born with a beautiful, healthy body and another is weak or deformed? What has a baby with physical problems done in his short life to deserve the body he was given?

Naturally, that baby has done nothing in his life to deserve his physical problems. He may be balancing karma he made in a previous life. However, it may not be because of karma at all. Sometimes a soul will volunteer before birth to be born with chromosome problems or other deformities or infirmities of the body in order to fulfill a specific purpose for God.

The law of karma and reincarnation enables us to better understand and to accept these seeming injustices in life. And we can be comforted to know that the law of karma is precise.

As we give our prayers and meditations for the souls of our children, we can learn to hold the concept in our hearts and minds of the perfect form and divine image of every soul. And we can spiritually prepare ourselves to accept the children we are given, regardless of their physical, mental or emotional imperfections. Thus for each child we receive we will be able to provide the greatest opportunity in life to fulfill his mission from God, no matter what that mission may be.

↜

When I was eight months pregnant with my second child, I had an ultrasound. I remember waiting in the specialist's examining room with my husband to hear the results. The doctor opened the door and said in a friendly voice, "You have a girl." And then I saw his face become more serious.

"Your daughter has a diaphragmatic hernia. That means she has a hole in her diaphragm and her organs are being pushed up into her chest cavity. We found her left kidney, stomach and heart under her left rib. Her heart is pushed up to the left and turned 90 degrees. She has a hole in her heart between the two lower chambers. Her left lung has not developed. And her intestines are not rotated properly.

"All those things are correctable if she doesn't have a chromosome problem. But because of her small size, I suspect she does. And if she does, she will die within a few minutes after birth—that is, if she survives the stress of labor. If she doesn't have a

chromosome problem, she will need a series of operations almost immediately after birth."

I was in shock. Without really being aware of anything after that, I allowed the doctor to perform an amniocentesis to confirm whether she had a chromosome problem. We were told we would have the answer within two weeks.

Ten days later, we found out our baby had trisomy 18, a chromosome problem the doctor had said was always fatal. As the days passed, I came to understand the prognosis. I then realized that all I `wanted was to be able to hold my baby in my arms while she was still alive.

I told about ten of my friends about our baby's problems, and I know they prayed for her. One mother did a daily novena of prayers. And a few people told me they were doing a rosary for her every day. I knew she was in God's hands.

Within a few weeks, I went into labor. The day before her birth we decided her name would be Catherine Anne. Because of her small size, Catherine was born very quickly. And to our amazement, she was alive!

I was in bliss as I held her—a precious soul in a tiny, flawed little body, trying so hard to have her chance at life. After a few hours, we realized that she was going to be with us for a while.

The next day, an X ray was taken to check Catherine's organs. That was the first time we realized what a living miracle she was. Her diaphragmatic hernia was gone! The left kidney was just slightly higher than normal. Her left lung had developed (and began functioning a week later). Her heart was in the normal place, although it still had multiple defects for which she received oxygen. The intestines were still rotated but functioned fine.

Catherine lived for only ten weeks. Even though her life was short, its quality was exceptional. She touched and changed the lives of many. I believe she came to teach us primarily about love, determination and courage. She helped me learn to trust God more, to love more selflessly and to be more compassionate. She made my life deeper and richer. I feel truly blessed to have known and cared for her.

The night Catherine died, my first daughter's six-year-old friend had a vivid dream. She was with Catherine on a cloud going up to the gates of heaven. Catherine's hair was no longer brown but golden and curly. Catherine looked up at the little girl and said, "I know you. You're Heather."

Heather saw Catherine dressed in a green robe with a green sash, and she had a little golden halo. She carried a tiny golden bow with golden arrows. At the tip of each arrow was a tiny pink heart. She carried a pouch of little pink hearts with her.

There was a lady on the cloud with them. Heather asked her who she was and the lady said she was Mary. Heather went into the gates of heaven with Catherine but then felt she had to come back to earth.

Heather waved good-bye to Catherine and started to go out the gate on the cloud. She felt something soft bump into her and dissolve. She turned around and saw Catherine with her little bow and arrows smiling at her. She realized that Catherine had shot love into her. She cried as she left, for Catherine Anne was like her own sister.

⤝

DNA MOLECULE MEDITATION

EXERCISE AND VISUALIZATIONS:

On the DNA molecule diagram on the following page, write the virtues and traits that you desire to see in yourself and your child. Then give violet-flame decrees and visualize this spiritual energy purifying the DNA molecule.

After giving violet-flame decrees, you can visualize the color vibrations of your heart flame infusing the DNA molecule. The three primary qualities of your heart flame are love (pink), wisdom (yellow) and power (blue).

PREAMBLE FOR VIOLET-FLAME DECREES:

In the name of God I AM THAT I AM and according to God's will, I decree for the purification of my DNA and of my child's DNA. I ask that it be infused with the following virtues and traits:_____

_____

_____

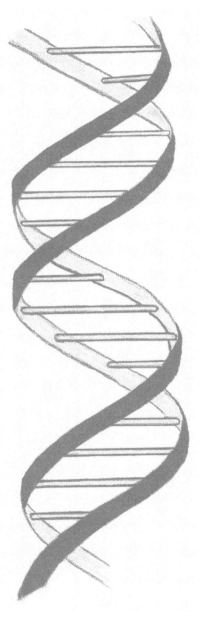

DNA Molecule

CHAPTER EIGHT

Meditations
to Convey Beauty
and Virtue
to Your Baby

Meditate on virtue within yourself,
and you will find the benefit of virtue.
Use it as the ground for the family,
and your virtue will last for generations.

—TAO TE CHING

In addition to using the violet flame to change your child's karma and genes, there are other ways you can increase his potential. Transmitting to your child in the womb particular talents, positive character traits, leadership abilities, and so on (even if you don't have these traits yourself) is a science you can master.

This science is one of the greatest phenomena in the universe. It is inspired by the parents' love for the child and their desire to give that child the greatest opportunity in life.

Meditation is an essential part of this science. In addition to the meditations previously mentioned, there are other very effective meditations you can do during pregnancy to help form the intricate patterns of thoughts and feelings, and even the physical cells and organs of your baby's body. These meditations can promote healthy development and impress beauty and perfection upon the soul and consciousness of your child.

The first type of meditation involves focusing on your unborn baby's current stage of development while giving the heart mantras and decrees at the end of this chapter. The second type uses classical music and art, as well as gems and nature scenes, to convey beauty and virtue to your baby.

〜

With my first pregnancy, I made a conscious effort to look at beautiful things. But with my second pregnancy, the desire to meditate on beautiful things was so incredibly strong that I knew it was coming from the soul of my baby. This child wanted beauty. He wanted me to focus on beauty every day. I even found myself searching through beautiful pictures in the middle of the night.

So throughout the pregnancy, I found myself looking at pictures of beautiful gardens and houses every day. And after our son was born, my husband began collecting pictures of beautiful houses.

This was such an unusual fixation for both me and my husband that I can only explain it as a great need for this soul. Though my son is now only three months old, I am anxiously waiting to see if he will become an architect or a landscape artist.

〜

Create a Meditation Book for Pregnancy

Just as the baby receives physical nourishment through the umbilical cord, so he receives spiritual light from the father's and mother's heart flames to sustain his life. The heart flames of the parents, primarily the mother, are the sponsoring light of the baby until he is born.

You can use visualizations and heart mantras to direct love and light from your heart into each cell of your baby's body before birth, while that body is being formed. The light you invoke as you give heart mantras passes through your heart and goes to the heart of the tiny body that is forming. And it goes to your child's soul, which is also participating in the creation of his body. When you use these heart mantras as a part of your meditation, you are infusing your baby's body with the Spirit of the living God.

These meditations are particularly important during the first trimester, when much of the organ development of the child takes place. For this reason, it's a good idea to practice these meditations on behalf of your child even before you know whether you have conceived.

One of the most exciting ways to participate in and influence your baby's development is by using a book of pictures on fetal development to meditate on your baby's growth week by week. You can purchase an illustrated book on fetal development for this purpose.[1] Or you can buy old science books or magazines, cut out the pictures and make your own meditation book.

To make your own meditation book, you can start by collecting photographs of the egg and sperm, the newly fertilized egg, the embryo and the fetus at the various stages through the nine months of gestation. Pictures of the fetal heart and developing brain from their formation to birth are also useful, as well as pictures of other fetal organs, molecules, cells and parts of cells.

Once you have collected and mounted these pictures in a notebook, you place your left hand to your heart and your right hand over the photograph of the embryo or fetus at your baby's current stage of gestation. You look at the photograph, you study it through the inner eye, and you memorize it as best you can so you can close your eyes and still see it. And as you are visualizing the baby in your womb, you can give the heart mantras and decrees.

If you memorize these mantras, you can place your full attention upon the visualization of the light passing through your heart, entering the heart of your baby and then enveloping his entire body. You can also place your hands upon the womb and use your hands as the instrument of that light and energy of love entering the child. So through your hands passes the light from your heart to the embryo or fetus at each stage of development. You can use the outline of fetal development at the back of this book (appendix A) to help you visualize your baby's stage of development as you meditate.

↩

I made a meditation book for my pregnancies.
It had pictures of saints, crystals and gems, scenic

*beauty and perfect geometry. Before my oldest son
was born I meditated on a replica of Michelangelo's
statue of David. My son now has a similar build.*

*I also kept a diary before my children were born
and still keep it. I write what I think they will enjoy
reading someday—how I felt when I was pregnant,
what it was like to care for them, what they are like
as individuals, and how they are uniquely special.
Mostly how much I love them.*

*I also prayed for their protection during each
stage of development. I daily visualized or looked at
pictures of a healthy baby in each stage of development and in the correct position at the later stages of
gestation. I also showed the pictures to my unborn
babies (by holding up the pictures in front of my
abdomen) and said to them, "This is how you are
supposed to be."*

*All three of my children were healthy and in the
correct position for birth, by God's grace.*

⤳

Meditation on Gems to Crystallize Virtues

You can include in your personal meditation book pictures of gems and their molecular structure. Gemstones
have a molecular structure that allows them to carry a
certain charge and energy vibration that corresponds to
particular qualities of God. Thus, for example, rose

CHART OF GEM QUALITIES

Color	Gems	Qualities
yellow	yellow diamond, yellow sapphire, topaz	wisdom, calmness, tranquillity, fidelity, strength, healing
green	emerald, jade, quartz crystal, diamond	healing, truth, memory, insight, clear vision, honesty, communication, precipitation
blue	diamond, sapphire, star sapphire, lapis lazuli	faith, power, clear thinking, strength, fortitude, courage, fearlessness, purity, protection
pink	ruby, diamond, garnet, rose quartz, pink beryl	love, compassion, courage, boldness, concentration
purple and gold	topaz, ruby, alexandrite, diamond with pearl	good cheer, love, peace, service, brotherhood
violet	amethyst, aquamarine, diamond	freedom, harmony, joy, transmutation, dignity, forgiveness, creativity, love
white	pearl, diamond, zircon, quartz crystal	discipline, purity, peace, protection, joy, order, hope, concentration

quartz holds the vibration of love, and emeralds hold the vibration of healing.

Through meditation upon gems we enter a very concentrated focus of God's energy. And the gem becomes the transmitter, or the transformer, of that energy to each cell of the little child through the mother's mind and attention.

So you can meditate on various gems for the crystallization of specific virtues you would like to see manifest in your child. This Chart of Gem Qualities will help you decide which gems to include as focuses of virtues in your meditation book.

You can also include in your meditation book pictures of flowers, nature scenes, angels and nature spirits, classical art and illustrations of the madonna and child.

⌒

My pregnancy was a very busy time, and I really did not have much time to do some of the meditations I wanted to do. But I did find one that was helpful and practical in the midst of my work schedule.

We had a rose garden at our house. Each day while driving to work with my husband in our rusty delivery van through a rather ugly warehouse district, I carried a beautiful rose and meditated on it. It transformed our commute, and I was able to have some very special meditations.

⌒

Classical Music and Art

The years from conception through age seven are the most creative period of the child's entire life. It is during this period that the intricate patterns of the soul and the four bodies of the child are established. To assist in the building of these intricate patterns, there is nothing that can replace meditation on the best classical music and art.

The unborn baby is profoundly sensitive and can perceive the beauty, virtue and joy that the mother sees and feels as she meditates upon beautiful works of art by masters such as Michelangelo, Leonardo da Vinci and Nicholas Roerich. As the mother meditates, the baby also learns to meditate, filling his consciousness with light and beauty.

Transmitting the beauty of art to the unborn baby stimulates the baby's soul to attune with her highest spiritual origins. And when the baby hears and feels divinely inspired music, his consciousness and the very atoms, cells and electrons of his four bodies will vibrate and coalesce around the patterns of this music.

↩

Much of my pregnancy was spent with a choir recording an album of devotional songs to the Blessed Virgin.[2] *My daughter now sings like a bird! She even sings like a trained singer—her pitch is right on and she holds the vowels a long time before singing the end consonant. And she loves the songs on the album!*

↩

The highest forms of music and art give double stimulus to the soul to attune with God and to contact the heart of beauty in nature. When the unborn baby is surrounded by beautiful music and art from conception, his outer senses are developed parallel to the inner senses of the soul. These meditations can also transfer to your baby inner keys to his own mission in life.

⁀

About a month before my daughter's birth, my husband found a stack of books on the arts and ballet. One book from the 1940s particularly stood out. It had beautiful pictures of Russian ballerinas and I meditated on them.

When my daughter was only one week old, I had a dream in which she was two or three years old. She said to me, "I'm a dancer, you know." Now at six, she really is a dancer. Recently she composed and then performed a Buddhic dance. I feel her mission is in the creative arts.

⁀

Meditation upon the best classical music influences virtually every mental and physical process. Music is especially key to the harmony of the emotional body— uplifting, calming, inspiring or relaxing, depending upon the specific piece.

Music is also an expression of beauty, and beauty is a universal medicine. Health and beauty are intimately related. And to preserve one, the other must be culti-vated. As a mother meditates upon the beautiful music of the master composers, she conveys to her child the beauty she perceives. As she elevates her consciousness by this music day by day, her overall feelings will ema-nate greater love and wholeness as well.

We know that the child in the womb learns through daily experiences with the mother's environment and culture. The child also learns through interactions with the world outside the womb through the vibrations of sound, light and movement.

↶

I taught ballet to children several times a week during my second pregnancy. In addition to classical music, I played uplifting, fun and happy music such as waltzes and Irish folk music to keep the children's interest.

Now my seventeen-month-old son loves to dance! He is very musical and rhythmic, and I could see these qualities even at nine months of age. He can tap his feet to a beat and clap or beat a drum to a rhythm. He starts to dance even when the music of the evening news comes on.

Just today he was saying "daeee" and kept repeating this and insisting that I stop what I was doing. I thought he was saying "Daddy," so we walked into the other room to look out the window to see if his daddy was there. But my son had a different idea. He held his hand up like he was asking me to dance, and it suddenly dawned on me that he was saying "dancing." So I picked him up and held his hand like we were dancing and we waltzed around the room.

৲

How Music Affects Body, Mind and Soul

From ancient China to Egypt, from India to the golden age of Greece, we find the same belief: music has the power to contribute to the sublime evolution or the utter degradation of the soul. Many of the great Greek philosophers, including Pythagoras, Plato and Aristotle, regarded music as indispensable to the health of the soul and influential in moral culture.

In *The Secret Power of Music*, David Tame states that there is scarcely a single function of the body that is not affected by musical tones. In addition, the effect of music on our emotions and desires is vast. Melodies cause a constant saga of tension and relaxation to occur within many parts of the body.

> Investigation has shown that music affects digestion, internal secretions, circulation, nutrition and respiration. Even the neural networks of the brain have been found to be sensitive to harmonic principles. . . .
>
> Researchers have discovered that consonant

and dissonant chords, different intervals, and other features of music all exert a profound effect upon man's pulse and respiration—upon their rate and upon whether their rhythm is constant, or interrupted and jumpy. Blood pressure is lowered by sustained chords and raised by crisp, repeated ones. . . .

Music affects the body in two distinct ways: directly, as the effect of sound upon the cells and organs, and indirectly, by affecting the emotions, which then in turn influence numerous bodily processes.[3]

The extent of music's influence over purely intellectual processes is just beginning to be recognized. Recent research is addressing the impact of sound on the brain. Certain kinds of classical music, by composers like Bach, Mozart and Beethoven, have been shown to have a range of positive effects on mental processes. These include expanding memory and speeding learning. Some believe that music can even raise IQ or change chromosomes.

What Constitutes "Good" or "Bad" Music?

As David Tame points out, music studies involving plants are particularly useful in demonstrating the effects of certain types of music on living organisms, since plants have no culturally induced preferences in music. Various studies have demonstrated that plants thrive when exposed to classical music and are stunted, damaged and even die when exposed to acid rock.

The philosophers and musicians of ancient civilizations claimed that certain types of music are inherently good and others are inherently bad. In other words, certain combinations of sounds are life-enhancing, while others are unhealthy and dangerous.

Therefore we come to the question, what constitutes "good" or "bad" music?

The answer is simple: good music gives life and bad music promotes death. And there is more to life and death than the two sides of the grave. The effect may be subtle, but it is also cumulative—involving the life or death of cells in the body. In addition, every moment that we listen to music may be enhancing or diminishing our soul's spiritual faculties and the life-energy in our spiritual centers, increment by increment.[4]

⌐⌐

With all of my children I played a lot of classical music during pregnancy. I simply couldn't tolerate hearing rock music. It would make me feel very stressed.

Now my children are very drawn to classical music. At four years old, my daughter asked a friend's mother if she had a Mozart tape to play. My two oldest daughters already write their own music.

> *They can pick music out on the piano and add*
> *their own chords to embellish it.*

↝

The 3/4 time of waltz music is closest to the human heartbeat. Therefore, it creates a sense of harmony within us when we hear it. Rock music, on the other hand, is not synchronized with the human heartbeat. In fact, it creates a type of static electricity that alters the heart rate.

The syncopated beat of rock music injures the chakras. When you hear rock music, your energy descends from the crown to the base chakra. Rock music may give you a temporary thrill, but it does not give you the currents of eternal life.

So it is important that pregnant women be very careful about the music they listen to and choose only life-enhancing music, since it affects the child within them. The period of a few months prior to conception and during pregnancy is a great time to take a course in classical music and start a collection of these recordings. (See appendix B at the end of this book for a list of favorite music selections that enhance life.)

Beethoven's Nine Symphonies
for the Nine Months of Gestation

In the splendor of his nine symphonies, Beethoven has traced steps whereby man progressively awakens to his divine destiny and rises majestically over his lesser self to a level of self-mastery. Each of his nine symphonies depicts some aspect of this great overcoming.

You can take Beethoven's first through ninth symphonies and use each as the emphasis for the corresponding month from conception to birth. It is very exciting to hear the unfoldment of life through these symphonies.

Beethoven's ninth symphony is a transcript of what he experienced at lofty levels of consciousness. The first three movements of this colossal symphony depict the passage of the spirit ascending through the three heavens. The final choral movement sounds the exaltation theme, which sweeps the soul into the very presence of God. The symphony as a whole gives expression to the supreme realization that all life is one and immortal.

As you listen to Beethoven's symphonies, just imagine the embryo or fetus being bathed in the vibration of freedom from these symphonies. This is an opportunity not to be missed!

HEART MEDITATION

VISUALIZATION:

Visualize a cord of light descending from your Higher Self through the crown of your head into your heart. The light of God will be released through your heart and chakras as you give the mantras and decrees on the following pages.

Visualize the light of God's love shining through your heart. As you say these mantras and decrees aloud, see that love as an intense fiery pink beam passing through your heart, entering the heart of your baby and then enveloping his entire body.

You can also place your left hand to your heart and your right hand over a photograph of an embryo or fetus at your baby's current stage of gestation. Then visualize your baby in the womb as you give the following heart mantras and decrees.

MANTRA:

Violet fire, thou love divine,
Blaze within this heart of mine!
Thou art mercy forever true,
Keep me always in tune with you.

Heart Meditation

I AM the light of the heart
Shining in the darkness of being
And changing all into the golden treasury
Of the mind of Christ.

I AM projecting my love
Out into the world
To erase all errors
And to break down all barriers.

I AM the power of infinite love,
Amplifying itself
Until it is victorious,
World without end!

THE HEART FLAME

DECREE:

O mighty threefold flame* of life,
Thou gift of God so pure,
Take my thoughts and energy
And make them all secure.

Under bond of brotherhood
And understanding fair,
Send thee forth unto my soul
The gift of holy prayer.

Communication's strands of love,
How they woo by heaven's law
A tender blessing for the good,
Releasing holy awe

(decree continues)

Threefold flame is another term for the heart flame. The heart flame is actually composed of three intertwining flames: the blue flame of power, the yellow flame of wisdom and the pink flame of love. These three flames also correspond to the Trinity: Father (Brahma), Son (Vishnu) and Holy Spirit (Shiva).

That draws me near the throne of grace
To now behold thy sacred face
And without fear dispense aright
The passions of pure God-delight
Which set me free from all that's been
The sinful nature of all men.

Christ, raise me to self-mastery,
The living passion of the free.
Determination, now arise
And lift me ever to the skies!

I AM, I AM, I AM
Enfolding life and being all
With the God-command
"Amen!" that shatters human pall.

I AM, I AM, I AM
The free—no bondage holds me back.
I AM the fullness of Love's law
Supplying every lack,
And consecration in full measure
Is my will and God's own pleasure.

DECREE:

I AM light, glowing light,
Radiating light, intensified light.
God consumes my darkness,
Transmuting it into light.

This day I AM a focus of the Central Sun.
Flowing through me is a crystal river,
A living fountain of light
That can never be qualified
By human thought and feeling.
I AM an outpost of the divine.
Such darkness as has used me is swallowed up
By the mighty river of light which I AM.

I AM, I AM, I AM light;
I live, I live, I live in light.
I AM light's fullest dimension;
I AM light's purest intention.
I AM light, light, light
Flooding the world everywhere I move,
Blessing, strengthening and conveying
The purpose of the kingdom of heaven.

CHAPTER NINE

Loving
Communication
with Your
Unborn Baby

By and large, the personality of the
unborn child a woman bears is a
function of the quality of mother-child
communication, and also of its specificity.
If the communication was abundant,
rich and, most important, nurturing,
the chances are very good that the baby
will be robust, healthy and happy.

—THOMAS VERNY

There's a tribe in Africa where the birth date of a child is counted not from when he's born nor even from the day of conception—but from the day the child is first a thought in the mother's mind.

So when the mother decides to have this child, she leaves the village and goes off to sit alone under a tree. There she sits and listens until she can hear the song of the child that she hopes to conceive. And after she's heard the song of this child, she goes back to the village and teaches it to the father. And so part of the time they are making love to conceive the child, they sing this song together to invite the child to join them.

Then when the mother is pregnant, she teaches the child's song to the midwives and the old women of the village so that throughout the labor and birth the child is greeted with his song. After the birth all the villagers learn the song, and as the child grows up they sing the song to the child whenever he falls or hurts himself. It is also sung in times of triumph or in rituals or initiations.

This song becomes a part of the marriage ceremony when the child is grown. And finally, at the end of his life, loved ones gather around the deathbed and sing this song to him as his soul gently leaves his body.[1]

Your Unborn Baby Can Communicate with You

One of the most touching communications I had with both of my babies while I was pregnant and especially right after they were born was that I found myself constantly humming a particular tune. For my first child the tune was "Greensleeves" and for my second child it was "Juanita."

The interesting thing is that I found these melodies very comforting to my babies after they were born. I guess that's when I started to realize the significance of the melodies. If my baby was agitated or crying, often just the humming of the tune would soothe him. Even though I had not thought about it too much at the time, I realized later that these melodies keyed into the unique identity of my children. Even though my children are much older now, the melodies are still meaningful to them and to me.

↫

Whether you tune in to the song of your child's soul or whether you simply have an awareness of the presence of that soul near you, you can communicate with her and she can communicate with you—even before conception.

I remember when I was a student at Boston University

and everywhere I went, whether I was sitting some-where or having a meal, I saw with my inner sight this blond, blue-eyed little boy hop up on a chair next to me. And I knew why he was there, but I wasn't ready to have children. So I'd say, "I can't have you now." And he kept coming back and coming back until finally I was married to Mark Prophet, and this soul became our firstborn son.

Now, what was that soul doing all of that time while he was in my presence?

He was studying the world. He was observing me. He was learning what I was learning. He participated in my intellectual training and also my spiritual training. Think about this. We can promote the intellectual and spiritual training of our children even before they are conceived.

So as soon as I knew that I was to have a child, which was usually quite some time before the conception of that child, I was in a talking, working, loving relationship with that soul. And it's very important that this never stop throughout life—that you have profound conversations with your children at all steps and stages of their lives.

⤶

My last child (my seventh) was a surprise, and I did not feel fully prepared for the coming of this soul. During the first few weeks of the pregnancy,

I alternately spoke with and sent thoughts to this little person in my womb, telling him that I wasn't rejecting him or unhappy to be pregnant but that I was trying to get myself over the shock of the pregnancy. I said I was trying to sort out my feelings and trying to get myself in gear to fully embrace the entire situation.

From time to time I would apologize to this soul for not being in the same rejoicing mode that was so natural during my other pregnancies. When I was about six weeks into the pregnancy, my husband was patting my tummy and telling me that he was sure the baby was a little girl. He started musing on some of his favorite female names.

Then I heard a tiny voice from somewhere say, "Don't be too sure!" Then he laughed a hearty laugh.

As the weeks and months of pregnancy passed, I learned to recognize that voice as the voice of my unborn son sounding in my inner ear. We had many talks together, mostly by telepathy, and we developed a rich and rewarding relationship during the entire prenatal period.

∽

When I was pregnant with my first child, my husband was very opposed to my teaching her about religion or spirituality. In frustration I prayed to God for help. Suddenly I felt my baby around me closely, enveloping me in a very loving and sweet feeling. And I heard her tell me: "Don't worry. Leave him to me. I can handle him. No problem."

I asked her, "Who are you?" Then I saw an image of a happy, fat Buddhist monk from Thailand, a wandering barefoot mendicant wearing homespun fabric.

From birth on, my daughter sat on my lap every morning for prayers and charmed her father so thoroughly that he never interfered. In fact, he began to pray too.

My daughter is now a very sweet and sensitive young adult who feels a deep connection to Southeast Asia.

↶

The soul of the unborn baby can communicate with the parents in many different ways, such as through dreams, intuitions or an inner voice. And sometimes the soul will convey to the parent an emphatic determination to fulfill her mission—especially when that mission is threatened.

↶

I was about twenty-six years old and unexpectedly pregnant with my third child. I had an IUD at the time. Abortion was not legal. My husband was upset about another pregnancy. I talked to the doctor, who said he would take out the IUD and this would

*terminate the pregnancy. So this was what we were
going to do.*

*I got in the car to go to the appointment and heard
a strong inner voice say, "I will not be killed!"*

*I was stunned. I turned around, went home and
called my husband. I said that I couldn't go through
with it—that I felt like I was killing someone.*

*So I gave birth to this child. And over the years as
this child has grown up, he has revealed a very strong
character. I can easily imagine him making such an
intense demand to not end his life.*

What Is Your Baby's Name?

According to Jewish legend, while the prophet Jeremiah
was still in the womb he cried, "I shall not leave it before
I receive my name." His father said, "I shall call thee
Abraham." But the unborn baby replied, "This is not my
name." The father continued to suggest names, but the
baby insisted that none of them fit him.

So the dilemma for the father of Jeremiah was that he
could not find the right name for his son. But the
prophet Elijah came to the rescue and proposed the
name Jeremiah. "This," said the unborn baby, "is my
name."[2]

⌒

*All three of my children's names flashed in my
mind when I was about three or four months preg-*

nant with my twins. The names that came to me for my twin boys were Francis and Tobias. And the name of the third child was Lalita.

I liked all the names at the time, but I kind of fought against the name Tobias because I was concerned everyone would call him Toby. I had this prejudice that Toby was just a naughty little boy's name, and I was trying to find a different name for him.

And then when he was born and they put him on my stomach, I heard a voice that said, "His name is Tobias." So I was obedient to that voice and named him Tobias.

And what I realize now is that the name really fits him. Even Toby fits him, because he is kind of mischievous at times. After the twins we also had a daughter, whom we named Lalita.

↩

One day I was really concerned about choosing the right name for my baby, and I thought to myself, "Well, I'll have to go through baby books." I was sitting on the edge of my bed and all of a sudden I was transported in my mind to a little room, and I was sitting on this stool at a big table like a ledger table. There was this huge book, about two feet by two feet, and it had a jeweled front cover. I was turning these huge pages and it had every name that was ever given to anybody—the name and the definition of the name and all the people who had the name.

And I was going through this big book and I thought, "Boy, this is going to take me forever!" In walked a young girl about twelve years old, with brown hair that was kind of wavy. She stood very stately and said, "My name is Cara June." And so I said "OK" and I closed the book, because that was all I needed to hear.

And then I was back in my room at the edge of my bed. I felt very elated and tingly for about three hours after that. When my daughter was born, I knew that it was the same child whom I had seen come into the room. So I named her Cara June.

↩

When one of my children was a baby of six months, I was shocked to feel the presence of another child "knocking on the door." I spoke with my husband about it and he had felt it, too. We agreed that we would tell the child to wait. This we did.

A few months later we felt the soul of this child asking to come again. Again we told her to wait. When our baby had become a toddler (I think he was fourteen months old), the child came a third time with a serene presence, not begging or badgering as I would have thought.

She beamed her name onto the screen of my

mind: Celeste Marie. *I think she knew that we could not resist her any longer once we had received that beautiful name. And she was right!*

When my husband came home from work I excitedly told him that the mysterious child had returned and given me her name. He told me he already knew it—she had visited him as well. We conceived her in joyous expectancy. And soon a picture of a beautiful rose came into my possession. This became the keynote for this child during pregnancy and birth. She is truly a very special rose—even now as a teenager navigating the rough waters of life.

❦

One way I developed a bond with my unborn child was through dreams. Although I had not been told the sex of the child, I knew intuitively she was a girl.

I had three dreams in which a little girl came to me at different ages, and one or two times she told me her name also. One time she said a name that didn't initially make an impression, but the next day I saw the same name in a different language and knew that this was the right name.

So I learned to be more sensitive as I communed with my child's soul and to pay attention to my dreams. And I've often shared with other expectant parents that when trying to decide upon the right *name for their child, I believe it is important to commune with the soul of the child. If something comes to you in a dream, it may be very significant. But if you are still not certain it is the right name, wait until the child is born. Then say the name softly and directly to the child, and watch for a sign or reaction from the child.*

↶

Talking to Your Unborn Baby

You form and reform your child by love, and love is communication by the Holy Spirit. And you form and reform your child by the power of your spoken words.

So it is important to talk to your baby (in soft, clear, loving words—not baby talk) as if he or she were already present. Your baby may or may not understand the meaning of the words, but he is surely affected by the feelings of love behind the words. Talking to your baby will help him feel welcome, and it will assist in his bonding to you.

↶

I talked to my babies when I was pregnant. With my last pregnancy, sometimes I would feel my son startle when I turned on the blender or vacuum cleaner. I would take care to rub my tummy and explain the loud startling sounds and tell him in a soothing voice that everything was OK. I got in the habit of warning my child before turning appliances on. When I did that, I did not feel him startle as much.

〜

When I was pregnant with my second child, I found out late in the pregnancy that my baby was in a breech position. Since my first baby was born by C-section, I knew that the obstetrician probably would not allow me even to attempt a normal delivery if this baby was breech.

So I talked to my midwife to find out what we could do to get the baby to turn upside down. He should have already been in the head-down position at that stage of my pregnancy.

She told me my options, and the only option I felt comfortable with was for me to try to coax the baby to change position. This involved lying upside down on an incline board and massaging my stomach in a circular motion while talking out loud to my baby, encouraging him to change position.

Well, my baby never changed position, and I found out later that it was probably because of the way the umbilical cord was wrapped around him. And he was delivered by C-section because it became apparent during labor that it would be unsafe for him to be born vaginally for a number of reasons. Interestingly, the surgery and recovery were very easy for me.

But the reward for all my coaxing and talking to my baby became apparent after birth. Within a few days I noticed that when my baby was fussing or crying, he would immediately respond to me when I talked to him in a soft, loving voice.

He would almost always stop crying and listen to me. Sometimes that was all that was needed to comfort him. And even if he was hungry, he would still stop crying and listen. I think only when he realized he was still hungry would he start crying again.

I was very intrigued by his response to my voice because I had not had the same experience with my first baby. I had communicated with my first baby during pregnancy through my thoughts, but I had not actually talked to him. It really was an amazing and rewarding experience to have this level of communication with my new baby.

❧

When I was pregnant with my twins, I found out that it is sometimes hard to have a natural childbirth with twins. But I wanted to have a natural childbirth, so I asked my midwife what would be the best position for them to be in for a natural birth. She said that in terms of possibly having less complications, it would be best if they were both head down. Well, at that time (I was about seven months pregnant), one of the twins had his feet down and the other one had his head down.

So I asked my midwife for some pictures of babies

in the correct position to meditate on. Then I went home, meditated on the pictures and asked the babies to both get into the head-down position.

I soon felt a big blip in my belly. When I went back to my midwife a week later for a checkup, both babies were head down. I was surprised because I thought it was going to take a long time for them to change position, but I just asked them once and they did it. And they stayed that way and were both born naturally, and I didn't have any complications.

❧

Talking to the unborn baby is one way the expectant father can have meaningful involvement in the child's life from the very beginning. In *The Secret Life of the Unborn Child*, Dr. Thomas Verny states that even though a man is at somewhat of a disadvantage in the bonding process (for obvious physiological reasons), the physical impediments are not insurmountable:

> Something as ordinary as talking is a good example: A child hears his father's voice in utero, and there is solid evidence that hearing that voice makes a big emotional difference. In cases where a man talked to his child in utero using short soothing words, the newborn was able to pick out his father's voice in a room even in the first hour or two of life. More than pick it out, he

responds to it emotionally. If he's crying, for instance, he'll stop. That familiar, soothing sound tells him he is safe.[3]

❦

Before our daughter was born, I talked to her all the time. Almost every night I said a little something to her. When she was born, the doctor put her on my wife's chest and our daughter looked around a bit. Soon after, I said hello to her and talked to her.

Then she did an amazing thing. She turned her head completely around, almost 180 degrees, to look at me, which was quite unusual for a brand-new baby. She seemed to want to see who was speaking because she recognized my voice. I was touched. It was a very precious moment for me.

❦

When every member of the family communicates with the baby in the womb, they begin to develop their own relationship with that baby. And the entire household becomes more sensitive to making the home the most harmonious and happy place for the baby's benefit. An uplifting household is also significant because many studies have shown that women who are happy during pregnancy are more likely to have intelligent and outgoing babies.

Education Begins in the Womb

In addition to making your baby feel welcome, talking to your baby stimulates brain development. Scientists tell us that after about the fourth month of pregnancy, a high percentage of the baby's brain cells die if they are not stimulated every day. The more we stimulate and the more we talk to the baby, the better it is for the baby's overall development.

～

When I was pregnant with my first child, I could tell that she was a very mentally active baby. I used to take long walks by the river and felt compelled to tell her about all the natural phenomena, like how the river came to exist (for example, that the water comes from springs and tributaries, which get their water from melting snow and rain, which comes from clouds, which get their moisture from evaporation, and so forth).

Now my daughter is five—and very smart. Everyone who meets her is impressed with her intelligence. And she is still intensely curious about everything around her—from what's on the news to why the dishwasher broke. So I haven't stopped talking to her and answering her questions.

～

For many years, I've known that education begins in the womb. I think I knew that long before I had my five children. In recent years, we've learned a lot more about the learning capacity of babies in the womb. Studies and firsthand stories reveal that the baby has a memory starting at the earliest months of gestation.

∽

When I was pregnant with my first son, I fainted in church. A friend helped me by lowering my head to the floor and it cleared up.

Four years later, I had a dizzy spell and once again leaned over to get my equilibrium. My son approached me, patted me on the back and said: "It's OK, Mommy. You'll be all right. Remember when you did this when I was in your tummy? I didn't like it because I was squooshed." And he laughed.

∽

There is an increased interest in and understanding of the importance of postnatal, and even prenatal, education. In my mind, this is the great revolution in education. And it is the open door whereby we can give children such love, such joy, such training, such self-esteem.

I believe that in all areas of prenatal and postnatal education, what we do as mothers and fathers—providing a stimulating environment, teaching our child and speaking to that child in the womb—awakens faculties that would otherwise die on the vine before the child was considered even capable of using those facul-ties for learning.

When I was carrying my fifth child, I would look at the letters of the Hebrew and Greek alphabets and make a mental image of those letters. I would then send the images to him while I said them aloud. I was specifically sending them through the crown chakra to the heart chakra, and I would visualize them on a screen for him to see.

I found that day after day he would be frolicking in the womb and having a happy time, and then I would sit down and say to him, "It's time for your lessons now." He would be totally quiet, very still. He would not move at all as I took him through his lessons on chem-istry, art, the Greek alphabet and the Hebrew alphabet. Then we would watch a video of a Japanese method of learning math.

After my son was born, we would show him these Japanese math videos, and we could tell that he knew he had seen them before. And to top that off, one day I had some Japanese journalists visit. While having lunch with them, I found out from these men that my son was saying Japanese words. He had been saying these words ever since he started talking, but I didn't know it because no one in my household spoke Japanese. So I realized that he had to have picked up these Japanese words from the videotapes he had heard in the womb.

This was one of the most exciting things I'd ever experienced. It shows us that education begins not only before birth but perhaps long before conception, when the angels bring to the mother and the father the notification that a soul is ready to be born.

⌒

My husband and I had been married for four months and were not thinking of having more children, as we already had seven between us. But our daughter had a different idea!

Several months before she was conceived, I was praying to Mary, the mother of Jesus, and heard inwardly a loud and clear voice of a young girl say, "That's me! That's my name. I'm Mary!"

Well, to say I was surprised is putting it mildly. A few months later, I became pregnant. Even before her conception, Mary's soul clearly conveyed to us her character. Her father says she "assumes the sale." She likes to push forward, announce herself and stir things up. She generally is a go-getter. She certainly did this with the way she announced her coming to us!

⌒

Before my husband and I had decided to have a second child, I felt the presence of a soul who was like a little cherub saying, "I'm waiting for you to have me." The thought just popped into my head one day while I was cooking. The baby knew that she would be born and she was letting me know.

It felt like this child was rambunctious, impatient and feisty—and I could tell this soul would enjoy life. I predicted she would be a chubby, jolly baby who sucked her thumb. And she was! She was born with her thumb in her mouth (almost) and had rolls of fat on her eight-pound, three-ounce body. All our friends said she was the happiest baby they'd ever known.

~

The Unborn Baby Knows the Mother's Feelings

Everything a pregnant woman does or feels affects her unborn baby. She finds out, sooner or later, that her unborn baby is alert and highly sensitive to auditory stimuli and to the emotional climate of her immediate environment.

Many firsthand stories of mothers verify this exquisite sensitivity. Babies kick a lot more when the mother is upset or in a disturbing situation, and they calm down dramatically when things are quieter and happier.

Often the expectant mother may not be aware of what she is communicating to her baby indirectly. But even her heart rate, temperature, respiration and muscle tension give the baby a very definite impression of what she is feeling. ~

My first pregnancy was very stressful. I was newly married and we had just started a business.

I was also quite insecure about the pregnancy and confused about the best ways to eat and take care of myself. When I had periods of greater strain, I could tell that the baby was more intense and active. The baby did not grow well during the first period of life, but eventually things got better.

This child was born with a strong sense of freedom but also had some fears and insecurities. This insecure part of him is intense, shy and fearful. I have a sense that my emotional state during pregnancy contributed to some of his emotional insecurity. Finally, at age seven, he seems to be overcoming some of his shyness.

In *The Secret Life of the Unborn Child*, Dr. Verny writes, "The unborn child is a *feeling, remembering, aware* being, and because he is, what happens to him—what happens to all of us—in the nine months between conception and birth molds and shapes personality, drives and ambitions in very important ways."[4] Through various studies Verny shows that there is a correlation between the mother's emotional state and the physical, mental and emotional development of the child.

He concludes that continual or long-term maternal stress or anxiety causes excessive maternal stress hormones to be secreted into the mother's bloodstream, which in turn can result in an overcharged autonomic nervous system in the baby. This may lead to low weight at birth, gastric disorders, reading difficulties and/or behavioral problems.[5]

❦

Before my first pregnancy, I had heard other mothers say how peaceful and happy they were during their pregnancies. I had also read several books that revealed the positive effects on the developing baby of a pregnant mother's joy and loving feelings.

Well, the circumstances of my first pregnancy were far from peaceful and joyful. My husband was working in another state. I found myself having to work sixty hours a week to pay bills and medical expenses. I was working in downtown Los Angeles and the smog was horrendous. My diet was primarily fast food. This was not exactly the ideal environment or nourishment for an unborn baby.

I also knew, at some level of my being, that I would have a C-section, which was frightening at the time. I was exhausted, stressed out and lonely. Many nights I found myself crying in bed. Sometimes I think it is only by the grace of God that I did not miscarry the baby.

The birth was indeed difficult—a 48-hour labor and a C-section. But of course, when I had my baby in my arms, it was all worth it! He had made it—

safe and sound! That's all that really mattered.

My newborn baby definitely showed, however, the effects of my emotional state during pregnancy. He was restless and underweight, and he would only nap for short periods of time. He startled easily and had a difficult time falling asleep unless I was nursing him or holding him. I felt sad about this for some time. But I knew all I could do was to move forward and to give this child abundant love and attention to help heal the emotional effects of this pregnancy.

A year after the birth of our first child, I was pregnant again. I was better prepared for this one emotionally, but the circumstances were not much better. I figured that the challenges during my pregnancies must have been some kind of karma returning. So I knew that I would have to really work hard during this pregnancy to keep myself happy and peaceful.

I had to daily affirm the positives in my life. After all, I did have much to be grateful for. For one thing, a few of my friends were not able to conceive. So I gave thanks and praise to God for the life in my womb. And I also talked to my baby frequently and told him how much I loved him and wanted him. Consequently, our second baby was entirely different. He was more peaceful and healthier at birth than our first child.

As the boys have grown up, our first child has struggled with low self-esteem and learning disabilities. My husband and I have had to work hard to help our son develop self-esteem in areas where he has been successful. Our second boy, in contrast, has always had a good sense of self-esteem and excels in school.

It is hard to say whether each child was simply born with these traits or whether they were the direct effect of my emotional state during pregnancy. But I believe it is a little of both. What I learned is that we do have karmic things to work out with our children—even during pregnancy. But as difficult as the circumstances may be, I believe we always have the choice to make things better and to give our children the support of our love and joy to help them overcome their own karmic challenges, as well as our own.

⟿

Love and Harmony in the Home

Love and harmony in the home prepare the spiritual cradle for the baby. When the relationship between the mother and the father is loving and harmonious, it is a great comfort to the unborn baby.

Therefore, if there are any short-term or long-term problems in getting along with your spouse, you can both decide to put them aside and say, "We will dedicate our love to this child no matter what our problems may be." One practical way to help you keep your commitment to be loving and harmonious, especially during pregnancy, is to keep your attention on the positive and virtuous aspects of your spouse and simply ignore the annoyances. Another is to use the decrees to the violet flame at the end of chapter 6.

In addition to being harmonious with your spouse, both parents can determine what they need to do to guard the love and harmony in their home. The father may see himself in the role of protector, not allowing anything to cross the threshold of the home that could cause unnecessary stress. Key sources of stress are financial worries, threats to the household from outside, problems with other children and problems in the marriage.

Every mother has to learn for herself what she needs to do to be happy and harmonious during pregnancy. Is it getting extra rest? Eating right? Having a clean house? Or perhaps it's taking an early morning walk, praying, listening to soothing or uplifting music, reading or talking with loved ones. Whatever you need, rearrange your life to fit it in.

↩

The initial joy and elation over learning I was pregnant helped carry me through the first rocky months of nausea and fatigue. I found that the best way to cope with that was to just "let go" and take the time to nurture and mother myself.

Once I passed through the first trimester, I felt livelier, healthier and more joyful than ever before. The second trimester was a wonderful time! Swimming and following a daily routine of yoga exercises specific for pregnancy were what helped me to stay in shape and feel good.

⌒

Many mothers find greater harmony by avoiding disturbing relationships, crowds and noisy places, television and movies. Each mother will find a different formula for creating her sense of happiness and well-being. This formula will help her establish an orderly routine and rhythm to her days. As a result of this harmony, more love and joy will naturally flow into her world.

⌒

I couldn't stand watching TV or movies. I was extremely sensitive during pregnancy and my heightened perception made it almost impossible to tolerate many of the movies I thought were OK before and after pregnancy. I think it's very important to avoid being bombarded by movies and TV during pregnancy. This kind of stimulation can be too much—I found that it inhibited my intuitive awareness of the thoughts and needs of my baby.

⌒

A mother's intuition about her baby—when the baby is to come, whether it is a boy or girl, what kind of personality he or she has and especially what the baby's needs are—is a special gift that mothers have had through the ages. What is not always understood is that fathers have this gift, too.

↶

My baby's due date came and went. He was three weeks late. He just didn't seem to want to be born. The doctor tried to induce labor and still nothing happened after about nine hours.

So my husband started talking to our unborn son saying: "Things down here really are nice. We are excited to meet you and to have you in our family. We are all ready for you."

After this gentle coaxing and reassurance, my labor finally started. Our son just needed his father to reassure him before he was ready to be born.

↶

Listen to your inner voice. And know that God will guide you in being the best mother or father to your precious one.

EPILOGUE:
YOUR BABY'S SOUL CAN BLOSSOM

It's hard to imagine what it's like to have a baby when you've never had one. The only way you can fathom it is to think of what you love most now—and then multiply that by infinity!

⌒

As every flower has the seed within itself to become a beautiful blossom, so every child has locked within himself the blueprint and the resources to fulfill his mission in life. Whether or not the flower blossoms depends upon the fertility of the soil, the brightness of the sun and the amount of rain. Whether or not the child realizes his peculiar genius and fulfills his mission depends to a large extent upon his environment in the womb and in the home.

As parents, you can create the most fertile environment for your child by preparing yourself spiritually to receive that child. This preparation begins ideally three months before conception—or even years earlier—

and it can influence your child's physical and spiritual inheritance.

But even more, I believe it is not enough to let your child inherit your bones or the chemistry of your blood or even your own measure of spirituality. As you prepare to receive your child, you can seek to draw forth from the star of that soul that shines above, awaiting the moment of birth, the substance of her Higher Self. The Higher Self is the star of perfection of each soul's individuality in God.

Thus you can enable the soul of your unborn child to be receptive to her own individuality by bringing into your environment the highest and most beautiful in art, in music, in literature, in drama and in nature. By giving the meditations in this book, you can convey beauty and virtue to your unborn child by the action of the flow of love through your heart chakra.

This flow of love welling up in your heart can make up the difference between any possible karmic or hereditary shortcomings of your unborn child and the perfection of his or her Higher Self. That gap between potential imperfections and future attainment can be filled in by the love of your heart.

This is where spiritual parenting begins. And it can continue throughout your entire life as you pursue greater levels of personal mastery, inner resolution with God, and the purification of body, mind, heart and soul.

With that love to protect the child throughout life, the fabric of that soul's evolution is strengthened, just as surely as the unfolding of the petals of the flower one by one creates the fullness of the floral offering.

The prayers and meditations in this book can bring to your child's soul a deep, lifelong connection to God. They endow the unborn child with the sacred qualities of grace, love and joy. This endowment is accomplished consciously by extending the spiritual fervor of your heart in devotion and visualization for what you desire to see manifest in your child.

Thus it is easy to understand the need for the purification of the heart as you prepare for your child, because it is through the heart that you will endow life with beauty, perfection and joy. And the conveyance of joy comes readily through the violet flame.

Invoking the violet flame is one of the most important spiritual exercises you can do for yourself and your child. Not only does the violet flame bring joy, but it can purify your four bodies and your chakras. And if you find that you have little time or energy for spiritual exercises, don't underestimate the benefit of even five minutes of violet-flame decrees a day.

The violet flame will enable you to balance karma with your child even before he joins your family. Thus, by the grace of the violet flame, you can clear the way for the most joyful and harmonious relationship possible with your child throughout your life. You can also commune with your child's Higher Self as you invoke the violet flame to assist in the balancing of his karma and in changing undesirable hereditary traits before birth.

The violet flame is indeed the transforming power of change. It is the greatest gift of love that you can give to the soul of your child, because it can help remove the obstacles to the unfoldment of your child's unique potential and mission in life. So prepare the fertile ground with love and joy and let that beautiful blossom of your child's soul come forth!

SUMMARY

Spiritual Preparation for Parenting
~
Ways to Nurture
Your Baby's Soul Before Birth

◆ Learn how to tend the needs of your own soul with sensitivity and kindness. Study and work on healing your soul psychology and seek professional counseling if needed.

◆ Seek resolution for any unresolved aspects of your relationship with your parents. Heal your soul by forgiving yourself, your parents or others who may have hurt you. You can give the prayer for forgiveness to assist in this process (page 37).

◆ Take periods of time alone to meditate on your heart and soul. Realize that you are loved perfectly by God. Know that your heart is your point of contact with God and the soul of your child-to-be.

◆ Experiment with giving five to fifteen minutes of violet-flame decrees daily for the healing and transformation of any physical or psychological problems you may have.

◆ Give the Violet-Fire Chakra Meditation for the purification of your chakras and for the transmutation of karmic debris (pages 62–64).

- Identify hereditary traits in your family that you do not want to pass on to your children. Invoke the violet flame to pass through your DNA chain for the transmutation of those traits.

- Ask God to send you a soul with specific virtues or talents, if you desire. Tell God what commitments you are willing to make for the sake of that child.

- Understand that marriage is a great opportunity for spiritual development and the balancing of karma. Have realistic expectations of your marriage partner and allow for flexibility and creativity in your roles.

- Choose a meditation for conception that uplifts you and your spouse to the heights of spiritual attunement. Seal your meditation each time you attempt to conceive and pray for the protection of conception (pages 80–88).

- Pray for inner strength as you prepare for the initiation of childbirth. Also pray for the protection of both mother and child—as well as the father, the midwife, doctors, nurses, hospital technicians and anyone else involved with the birth.

- Begin a talking, working, loving relationship with the soul of your child-to-be, even before conception. Your child's soul can communicate with you in many different ways, such as through dreams, intuitions or an inner voice. Listen for that still small voice.

- Prepare a spiritual cradle for your baby by maintaining a loving and harmonious environment in your home. The mother can find a unique daily routine for creating her sense of happiness and well-being. The father can offer prayer support and protect his wife from situations that could cause unnecessary stress.

- Teach your baby in the womb by talking to him as an intelligent and mature soul and by providing a stimulating environment. You can even give him academic or cultural lessons, if you choose.

- Give the Meditation for Protection daily to guard the healthy development of your baby from conception through birth (pages 108–10).

- Offer specific prayers during each trimester, asking God to assist the soul of your child to transmute her negative karma and any weaknesses in her mental, emotional and physical bodies (pages 126–29).

- Give violet-flame decrees for the purification of your child's etheric body (ideally three months before conception). Visualize the perfection of your child's soul when it was created by God (pages 130–34).

- Maximize your child's hereditary potential by giving the DNA Molecule Meditation. Visualize the violet flame purifying and infusing your DNA and your child's DNA with virtuous qualities (pages 149–50).

- Give the Heart Meditation, using pictures of the developing fetus, to direct love and light from your heart into every cell of your baby's body at each stage of prenatal development (pages 168–72).

- Meditate on classical art and music (especially Beethoven's nine symphonies) for building the intricate patterns of the soul and the four bodies of your child. Begin a collection of music selections to enhance life (see appendix B).

Appendix A:
Outline of Fetal Development

During the embryonic period (the first 2 months) all the baby's major body structures and organs begin to form. Since there are so many rapid changes, these developments are listed in this section week by week. The developments for the fetal period (months 3 through 9) are significant but relatively slower and are therefore listed month by month.

The Embryonic Period: Weeks 1 through 8*

WEEK 1

* The ovum is fertilized by one sperm, and the chromosomes of the sperm and ovum intermingle. Each parent supplies 23 chromosomes, combining to make 46 chromosomes.

* Over the next 2 to 3 days, the fertilized cell undergoes rapid division and, while traveling down the Fallopian tube, becomes a 9- to 12-cell embryo.

---

*Medical providers usually describe weeks of pregnancy from the beginning of the last menstrual cycle. This is two weeks earlier than the actual fertilization, which is when the fetal age is determined. So if your doctor tells you that you are ten weeks pregnant, the fetal age is eight weeks. For consistency, fetal age is used throughout this section (as well as in chapter 5).

- By day 7, the embryo enters the uterus and attaches to the uterine lining.

WEEK 2

- The implanted embryo embeds more deeply into the uterine lining.

- The amniotic cavity and placenta (which transports nutrients and oxygen to the baby) begin to develop.

- Three different layers of cells, called germ layers (ectoderm, mesoderm, endoderm), will generate into the specialized organs and tissues.

WEEK 3

- The baby's length is about 1.5 mm (.06 inch).

- A pair of heart tubes (which will become the baby's heart) is formed. This pair is fused and begins to beat some time between days 22 and 27! Blood vessels first appear and will form a primitive cardiovascular system.

- The future central nervous system (brain and spinal cord) is being created.

- The baby's skeleton is starting to form.

Note: Weeks 4 through 8 of the embryonic period are very critical. All major body structures begin to form, and by the end of week 8 all the major organs have started to develop. This is an extremely important period of development because the embryo is most vulnerable to factors that can interfere with healthy development.

WEEK 4

- The baby grows rapidly and is 2 to 4 mm (about .1 inch).

- The major divisions of the central nervous system are established—forebrain, midbrain, hindbrain and spinal cord.

- The eyes and ears begin to form.

- Four pairs of brachial arches, later to become the intricate parts of the face and neck, have formed.

- Lungs, kidneys and digestive tract are developing.

- Limb buds are forming.

WEEK 5

- The baby has a big growth spurt this week. At the beginning of the week, he is 4 to 5 mm long (less than ¼ inch) and by the end of the week is 11 to 13 mm (about ½ inch).

- Five distinct divisions of the brain can now be discerned. The two cerebral hemispheres have formed and are growing rapidly.

- Eyes, ears and nose structures continue to form.

- The beating heart has divided into right and left chambers. Blood is beginning to be pumped by the heart through the circulatory system.

✦ Air passages (bronchi) for the lungs are forming.

✦ The intestines, appendix, pancreas and spleen are developing.

✦ Limb buds continue to take shape. Plates that will form the hands and feet are present.

WEEK 6

✦ The baby's size is around 13 to 20 mm (½–¾ inch).

✦ The heart has its distinct shape; aortic and pulmonary heart valves have developed.

✦ The lungs have definitive lobes and the bronchi are branching into small airways.

✦ Elbows are now present and the arms and legs are longer and extend forward. Hand and foot rays, which will become fingers and toes, have formed.

✦ The eyelid folds are forming.

✦ The external ears develop from skin folds, and the vestibular system in the inner ear begins to form.

✦ The upper lip and tip of the nose are formed.

✦ Primitive teeth and the palate are emerging.

WEEK 7

◆ The baby is 22 to 30 mm long (about 1 inch).

◆ The baby's face now has eyes, nose, lips and tongue.

◆ The optic nerve, a nerve connection from the eye to the brain, is developing. The pupil of the eye also forms this week.

◆ The digestive organs are attaining their final shape and positions.

◆ The external genitalia are forming.

◆ Muscles are growing rapidly throughout the body and begin to move spontaneously.

◆ The limbs undergo great change during this week and begin their first tiny movements.

◆ Notches appear on the digital rays, indicating future fingers and toes.

WEEK 8

◆ The baby's size is 31 to 42 mm (1 to 2 inches).

◆ The eyes are starting to move toward the middle of the face during weeks 8 to 10. The eyelids are fused and stay closed until week 25.

◆ The cerebral cortex of the brain begins to acquire its specific cells.

- Lung airways (bronchi) continue to branch.

- The digestive tract becomes more complex.

- Definitive muscles of the head, trunk and limbs enable the baby to move.

- The baby can now breathe and swallow.

The Fetal Period: Weeks 9 through 38

WEEKS 9 THROUGH 12 (MONTH 3)

- The baby, now called a fetus, is about $1\frac{3}{4}$ to $2\frac{1}{2}$ inches long and is rapidly growing.

- The brain has its general structural features. The pituitary gland is beginning to make hormones.

- The lungs have taken their definite shape and primitive breathing motions of the mouth begin.

- The liver is the main site of producing red blood cells. By 12 weeks, this also occurs in the spleen.

- The kidneys begin to produce urine.

- The fetal pancreas is developing.

- The genitalia are well defined by 12 weeks and the baby's sex can be identified.

- The face is broad and eyes are widely separated with the lids fused shut. During weeks 11 to 12, the eyes move to the front of the face and the ears migrate from the neck to the head.

* By week 12, the skeletal system is beginning to ossify (to absorb calcium and harden).

* Fingers and toes have separated, and the nails are growing.

* Maturing muscle development now allows the baby to stretch, rotate, curl, grasp and swallow.

WEEKS 13 THROUGH 16 (MONTH 4)

* The baby gains weight and grows rapidly during these weeks. By week 16, the baby is about 5 to 5½ inches long.

* Parts of the brain, such as the cerebellum and the two hemispheres, are better defined.

* Heart cardiac muscle is more condensed.

* Organs and tissues such as tonsils, adenoids, sinuses, special lung cells, kidneys and bones continue to refine.

* The external ears are in the correct position and stick out from the head. Reactive listening may begin as early as week 14.

* Sweat and sebaceous glands appear in the skin.

• During week 15, the baby's body begins to produce fat, an important part of metabolism and heat production.

• Fine hair, called lanugo, covers the baby's body.

• Fingernails and toenails are well formed.

• Fetal movements are more spontaneous, coordinated and complex. (Fetal movement is usually felt by the mother when the baby is 14 to 18 weeks.)

WEEKS 17 THROUGH 20 (MONTH 5)

• By week 17, the baby is about 5 to 6 inches long and weighs ½ pound. The baby's weight will increase fifteenfold between now and birth!

• From 18 weeks to term, blood-cell formation increases in the bone marrow and decreases in the liver. The liver also helps break down the by-products of red blood cells (bilirubin).

• By week 19, the development of the digestive system enables the baby to swallow and absorb amniotic fluid. Unabsorbed material (meconium) now passes as far as the large bowel.

• Sebaceous glands and skin cells form an oily coating that protects the new skin of the baby.

◆ Eyebrows and eyelashes start to form. Eyelids are well developed and the eyes are still closed.

◆ The nose and ears ossify in week 20.

◆ Tooth enamel is deposited around week 20.

WEEKS 21 THROUGH 25 (MONTH 6)

◆ During week 21, the fetus weighs about 1½ pounds. It grows to more than 2 pounds by 25 weeks. Miraculously, the baby has a chance of living if born at this time.

◆ The baby's body is well proportioned (the head is about one-third of the body length) and has a lean appearance with wrinkled skin.

◆ The cerebral cortex has developed layers.

◆ The inside walls of the lungs produce a substance that keeps the lungs open while developing.

◆ During week 21, rapid eye movements are detected, indicating some sort of dreaming activity.

◆ Eyelids open during weeks 25 to 26, and they begin to blink.

◆ Vision is maturing. The retina, where light images come into focus, is developing layers.

WEEKS 26 THROUGH 29 (MONTH 7)

◆ At 26 weeks, the baby is about 2½ pounds and 10

inches long. By week 29, he or she will be 3½ pounds and 18 inches long.

◆ The baby is getting more plump, collecting fat, and skin wrinkles begin to smooth out.

◆ At about 26 weeks, the brain forms grooves and indentations, and the amount of tissue increases.

◆ Specific cerebral cortex fissures and convolutions rapidly appear in week 28.

◆ The central nervous system can direct breathing movements and control body temperature.

◆ The lungs are now capable of breathing air.

WEEKS 30 THROUGH 34 (MONTH 8)

◆ At week 30, the baby is about 4 pounds and 16 to 19 inches long. The baby will gain about ½ pound per week from now until birth.

◆ The brain continues to grow and refine.

◆ The digestive tract and lungs are reaching full maturity.

◆ The testes descend into the scrotum during weeks 28 to 32.

◆ A pupil light reflex can be elicited by week 30. The baby can sense the difference between light and dark through the abdominal and uterine walls.

- Taste buds can differentiate more tastes.

- The skin is smoother and less red.

WEEKS 35 THROUGH 38 (MONTH 9)

- The baby is now about 6½ to 7 pounds and 21 to 22 inches long.

- This finishing period is devoted to building tissue and preparing the organs (primarily the lungs and heart) to function outside the uterine environment. The last organ to mature is the lung.

- The head is smaller now in relation to the rest of the body (¼ the total length of the baby) but is still one of the largest areas.

- The functions of the central nervous system are refined.

- Fat is developing rapidly in the final 6 to 8 weeks of gestation.

Appendix B:
Favorite Music Selections

Adolphe Adam   -"O Holy Night"

Johann S. Bach   -"Sheep May Safely Graze"
                            -"Jesu, Joy of Man's Desiring"
                            -"Sleepers Awake!"
                            -Magnificat in D Major
                            -Toccata and Fugue in D Minor
                            -Passacaglia and Fugue in C
                             Minor
                            -Air from Suite no. 3 in D
                            -*Mass in B Minor*

Bach-Gounod   -"Ave Maria"

Ludwig van Beethoven
                            -Symphonies no. 1 through no. 9
                            -Piano Concerto no. 5
                             ("Emperor")

Johannes Brahms   -"Lullaby"

Ernst Eichner   -Andante from Concerto in
                             C Major for Harp and Orchestra

Edward Elgar   -"Pomp and Circumstance,"
                             nos. 1 and 4

-Variations on an Original
Theme ("Enigma"), op. 36 no. 9

STEPHEN FOSTER

-"Beautiful Dreamer"

CÉSAR FRANCK

-Symphony in D Minor
-"Panis Angelicus"

GIOVANNI GABRIELI

-A *Capella Mass*
-Canzonas and Sonatas

CHARLES GOUNOD

-"Soldier's Chorus" from *Faust*
-*St. Cecilia Mass*

EDVARD GRIEG

-"In the Hall of the Mountain
King" and "Morning Mood"
from *Peer Gynt*, suite no. 1 op. 46
-Concerto no. 1 in A Minor
-"The Last Spring" from *Two
Elegiac Melodies*

GEORGE F. HANDEL

-*Messiah*
-"Largo" from *Xerxes*
-"Thanks Be to Thee"
-"See, the Conquering Hero
Comes!" from *Judas Maccabaeus*

FRANZ LEHÁR

-"Thine Is My Heart Alone" from
Land of Smiles

FRANZ LISZT

-Liebestraum no. 1

-"Resurrected," "Easter Hymn,"
and "March of the Three Kings"
from *Christus*
-Concert Etude no. 2 in F Minor
-"Benediction of God in Solitude"

EDWARD MACDOWELL   -"To a Wild Rose"

ALBERT MALOTTE   -"The Lord's Prayer"

PIETRO MASCAGNI   -Intermezzo from *Cavalleria Rusticana*

JULES MASSENET   -Meditation from *Thais*

FELIX MENDELSSOHN   -"Wedding March" from *Midsummer Night's Dream*
-"War March of the Priests"
-"On Wings of Song"

WOLFGANG A. MOZART   -Symphony no. 41 in C, K. 551 ("Jupiter")
-"Die Zauberflöte," Act 1
-"Eine Kleine Nachtmusik," K. 525: I Allegro

JOHANN PACHELBEL   -Canon in D Major

GIOVANNI PALESTRINA   -*Pope Marcellus Mass*
-*Missa Brevis*

AMILCARE PONCHIELLI   -"Dance of the Hours" from
                        La Gioconda

GIACOMO PUCCINI   -"O Mio Babbino Caro" from
                        Gianni Schicchi
                       -"Love Duet," "Humming
                        Chorus" and "One Fine Day"
                        from *Madame Butterfly*

SERGEI RACHMANINOFF   -Concerto no. 2 in C Minor
                       -Rhapsody on a Theme of
                        Paganini, 18th variation
                       -Vocalise, op. 34 no. 14

NIKOLAI RIMSKY-KORSAKOV
                       -"Song of India"
                       -"Procession of the Nobles"
                        from *Mlada*

SIGMUND ROMBERG   -"Golden Days of Youth"
                       -"One Alone" from *The Desert Song*

CAMILLE SAINT-SAËNS   -"The Swan"

FRANZ P. SCHUBERT   -"Ave Maria"
                       -*German Mass*

JEAN SIBELIUS   -"Finlandia"
                       -Karelia Suite, op. 11;
                        III Alla marcia

BEDRICH SMETANA   -"The Moldau" and "Vysehrad"
                        from *Ma' Vlast* (My Fatherland)

JOHANN STRAUSS
-"Emperor Waltz"
-"Vienna Blood"
-"Blue Danube Waltz"
-"Tales from the Vienna Woods"

PETER I. TCHAIKOVSKY
-Piano Concerto no. 1
in B-flat Major
-String Quartet no. 1 op. 11;
Andante Cantabile

RALPH VAUGHAN WILLIAMS
-"Lark Ascending"
-"Fantasia on a Theme
by Thomas Tallis"
-"Five Variants on Dives
and Lazarus"
-"Fantasia on Greensleeves"
-*Mass in G Minor*

GIUSEPPE F. VERDI
-"Celeste Aida" and "Triumphal
March" from *Aida*

ANTONIO VIVALDI
-*The Four Seasons*

RICHARD WAGNER
-Preludes to Acts 1 and 3, and
"Bridal Chorus" from *Lohengrin*
-Overture from *Rienzi*
-Prelude from *Die Meistersinger*
-Prelude to Act 1 and "Good
Friday Spell" from *Parsifal*
-"Forest Murmurs" from *Siegfried*

-"Dawn and Siegfried's Rhine
-Journey" from *Götterdämmerung*
-Prelude from *Tristan and Isolde*
-"Magic Fire Music" and "Entry of
the Gods into Valhalla" from
Das Rheingold
-"Evening Star" and Overture
from *Tannhauser*

Notes

Chapter 1: *Your Child Has a Mission*

Title page quotation: William Wordsworth, "Ode: Intimations of Immortality from Recollections of Early Childhood," stanza 5.

1. Mahabharata 13.6.6, in Christopher Chapple, *Karma and Creativity* (Albany: State University of New York Press, 1986), p. 96.

2. Gal. 6:7. All Bible verses are from the King James Version unless otherwise noted.

3. Matt. 7:2, 12 (New Revised Standard Version).

4. Helen Wambach, *Life Before Life* (New York: Bantam Books, 1979).

5. Joel L. Whitton and Joe Fisher, *Life Between Life* (New York: Warner Books, 1986), pp. 43, 44.

6. Wambach, *Life Before Life*, pp. 163, 164.

Chapter 2: *Prepare for Your Child by Healing Your Soul*

Title page quotation: Kahlil Gibran, *The Prophet*.

1. For more information on your Higher Self, see Elizabeth Clare Prophet, *Access the Power of Your Higher Self* (Corwin Springs, Mont.: Summit University Press, 1997).

2. Prov. 22:6.

3. Sidney B. Simon and Suzanne Simon, *Forgiveness: How to Make Peace with Your Past and Get On with Your Life* (New York: Warner Books, 1990), p. 21.

4. *Kuan Yin's Crystal Rosary: Devotions to the Divine Mother East and West* directed by Elizabeth Clare Prophet, published by Summit University Press, 3-audiocassette album of hymns, prayers and Chinese mantras that invoke the merciful presence of Kuan Yin.

5. *A Child's Rosary to Mother Mary*, 15-minute scriptural rosaries for children and adults, available on CD and audiocassette through Summit University Press.

Chapter 3: *A Unique Spiritual Energy for Healing and Transformation*

Title page quotation: Psalm 91:14, 15 (Jerusalem Bible).

1. Dr. Alfred A. Tomatis, quoted in Tim Wilson, "Chant: The Healing Power of Voice and Ear," in *Music: Physician for Times to Come*, ed. Don Campbell (Wheaton, Ill.: Theosophical Publishing House, Quest Books, 1991), p. 13.

2. Josh. 6:20; Matt. 8:16; Mark 9:25; Acts 3:6.

3. John Woodroffe, *The Garland of Letters* (Pondicherry, India: Ganesh and Co., n.d.) pp. 4–5.

4. John 1:1; Gen. 1:3.

5. Exod. 3:13, 14.

6. See also Elizabeth Clare Prophet, *Violet Flame to Heal Body, Mind and Soul* and *The Creative Power of Sound*. For an audiocassette of violet-flame decrees, see *Save the World*

with Violet Flame! 1. Wallet-size color pictures of each of the chakras also available. To order books, audiocassette and wallet cards listed here, contact Summit University Press.

Chapter 4: *How to Spiritualize Marriage and Conception*

Title page quotation: *Iggeret ha-Qodesh,* quoted in Daniel C. Matt, *The Essential Kabbalah: The Heart of Jewish Mysticism.*

1. Gen. 2:24.

Chapter 5: *The Miracle of Life from Conception Through Birth*

Title page quotation: Julian S. Huxley, quoted in Maria Montessori, *The Absorbent Mind.*

1. Maria Montessori, *The Child in the Church,* ed. E.M. Standing (St. Paul: Catechetical Guild Educational Society), p. 13.

2. See also Elizabeth Clare Prophet, *How to Work with Angels,* booklet; *Devotions, Decrees and Spirited Songs to Archangel Michael,* 70-minute audiocassette, Summit University Press.

Chapter 6: *You Can Help Change Your Child's Karma*

Title page quotation: Maria Montessori, *The Child in the Church.*

Chapter 7: *Spiritual Heredity*

Title page quotation: R. Swinburne Clymer, *How to Create the Perfect Baby.*

1. *Encyclopaedia Britannica*, 15th ed., s.v. "genetics and heredity."

2. II Tim. 1:5.

Chapter 8: *Meditations to Convey Beauty and Virtue to Your Baby*

Title page quotation: *Tao Te Ching*, chap. 54, trans. Man-Ho Kwok, Martin Palmer and Jay Ramsay.

1. For beautiful color photographs of the developing fetus, see Lennart Nilsson, Mirjam Furuhjelm, Axel Ingelman-Sundberg and Claes Wirsén, *A Child Is Born* (New York: Dell Publishing, 1977).

2. *Sanctissima: Music for World Peace*, 19 beautiful hymns to the Blessed Virgin Mary, choir conducted by Elizabeth Clare Prophet, 70-minute album, available on CD and audiocassette through Summit University Press.

3. David Tame, *The Secret Power of Music* (Rochester, Vt.: Destiny Books, 1984), pp. 136, 137. Used by permission of the author.

4. Ibid., pp. 142–44.

Chapter 9: *Loving Communication with Your Unborn Baby*

Title page quotation: Thomas Verny, M.D., *The Secret Life of the Unborn Child*.

1. Jack Kornfield, *A Path with Heart: A Guide Through the Perils and Promises of Spiritual Life* (New York: Bantam Books, 1993), p. 334. Used by permission of the author.

2. Louis Ginzberg, *The Legends of the Jews,* vol. 6 (Philadelphia: The Jewish Publication Society of America, 1956), p. 385.

3. Thomas Verny, M.D., with John Kelly, *The Secret Life of the Unborn Child* (New York: Dell Publishing Co., 1981), p. 31.

4. Ibid., p. 15.

5. Ibid., pp. 59, 91.

Reflections

_____

_____

_____

_____

_____

_____

_____

_____

_____

_____

_____

_____

_____

_____

_____

_____

_____

_____

_____

_____

_____

_____

_____

Reflections

Reflections

Reflections

Reflections

Reflections

Other titles from
SUMMIT UNIVERSITY 🔥 PRESS®

Reincarnation:
The Missing Link in Christianity

The Human Aura

The Answer You're Looking for Is Inside of You

How to Work with Angels

The Creative Power of Sound

Access the Power of Your Higher Self

Violet Flame to Heal Body, Mind and Soul

Summit University Press titles are available from fine book-stores everywhere, including Barnes and Noble, B. Dalton Bookseller, Borders, Hastings and Waldenbooks.

For information about seminars and conferences with Elizabeth Clare Prophet or for a free catalog of books and tapes, write to Summit University Press, P.O. Box 5000, Corwin Springs, Montana 59030-5000 U.S.A.
Fax 1-800-221-8307 (406-848-9555 outside the U.S.A.)
Visit our Web site at http://www.tsl.org or
E-mail us at tslinfo@tsl.org

ELIZABETH CLARE PROPHET is a pioneer of modern spirituality and the mother of five children. She has written a number of books, including *Reincarnation: The Missing Link in Christianity*, *The Lost Years of Jesus*, *Forbidden Mysteries of Enoch*, *The Human Aura* and *Kabbalah: Key to Your Inner Power*.

Mrs. Prophet has lectured throughout the United States and the world on spiritual topics, including angels, the aura, soul mates, prophecy, parenting, spiritual psychology, reincarnation and the mystical paths of the world religions.

She has been featured on NBC's *Ancient Prophecies* and has talked about her work on *Donahue*, *Larry King Live*, *Nightline*, *Sonya Live* and *CNN & Company*. She lives in Corwin Springs, Montana.

NANCY HEARN has been an editor and children's book writer with Summit University Press since 1991. She has also taught preschool and developed religious education materials for children. She is the mother of two young boys.

JOYE BENNETT has a doctorate in psychology, specializing in children and families. She also earned a master's degree as a child health associate/physician's assistant in 1979. With her combined training in pediatrics and child psychology, she has taught parenting workshops and provided care to hundreds of new parents and their children.